Freedom To Fall

BY

CAROL

HAMPSON

ISBN: 978-1-4525-5563-8 (sc)
ISBN: 978-1-4525-5562-1 (e)

Balboa Press books may be ordered through booksellers or by contacting:

Balboa Press
A Division of Hay House
1663 Liberty Drive
Bloomington, IN 47403
www.balboapress.com
1-(877) 407-4847

Because of the dynamic nature of the Internet, any web addresses or links contained in this book may have changed since publication and may no longer be valid. The views expressed in this work are solely those of the author and do not necessarily reflect the views of the publisher, and the publisher hereby disclaims any responsibility for them.

Library of Congress Control Number: 2012913097

The author of this book does not dispense medical advice or prescribe the use of any technique as a form of treatment for physical, emotional, or medical problems without the advice of a physician, either directly or indirectly. The intent of the author is only to offer information of a general nature to help you in your quest for emotional and spiritual well-being. In the event you use any of the information in this book for yourself, which is your constitutional right, the author and the publisher assume no responsibility for your actions.

Printed in the United States of America

Balboa Press rev. date: 8/8/2012

IN LOVING MEMORY
OF
CHRISTOPHER

Contents

"Young Climber Happiest when Scaling New Heights" 7
The trees in the forests are the disciples
                     by Chris Hampson 11

1   The Fall 13

2   The Eagle Flies 19

3   Mother and Son ....,,31

4   Spirit of the Mountains 45

5   The Fire of Life ....,61

6   Love of Climbing 73

7   True Freedom 83

8   Yosemite 95

9   At Overhang Bypass 115

10   Beyond the High Sierra 125

11   "We Take These Risks" 137

Epilog: Stone Steeple 149

Glossary: Climbing Terms 153

Acknowledgments 157

Chris in El Cap Meadow, Yosemite National Park, May 2003.

Young Climber Happiest when Scaling New Heights

By Claire Martin, Denver Post Staff Writer

Sunday, June 8, 2003

Breckenridge climber Chris Hampson was on his way to heaven, 950 feet up a gorgeous wall on Lower Cathedral Peak in Yosemite National Park, when he took the fall that caused his death on May 31. He was 25.

Hampson fell in love with rock climbing when he was 14. "That was the moment his life changed," said his mother, Carol Hampson. His father, Alan Hampson, agreed that Chris found his path in life when he discovered climbing.

Chris Hampson and Greg Van Dam, his best friend and longtime climbing partner, learned to climb with a small group of campers at Geneva Glen, a camp in Indian Hills. Once they got the hang of it, the two often sneaked away from the camp's organized activities so they could practice climbing moves on the boulders nearby.

"After that, we climbed everywhere," said Van Dam, who met Hampson to climb in Canyonlands National Park shortly before Hampson went on to Yosemite.

When they were learning to climb, one of their favorite proving grounds was on the granite slabs and cracks above the South Platte River, between Conifer and Sedalia. The first climb that Hampson led was on the Cynical Pinnacle, a classic granite dome that's a favorite among climbers.

"He'd say, 'C'mon, we can do it! I'll lead the hard pitch!' Van Dam remembered. "He brought me up so many things, from Cynical Pinnacle to the tower we did in Canyonlands last month. He was really an inspirational, courageous climber. For him, climbing was all about the journey and not the destination. He just loved moving over stone."

Nothing could keep Hampson away from the rock, especially once he began figuring out how to balance on little more than a crystal nub and a thin hard flake.

"It was his passion," his mother said.

"Even when he was little, he had this fascination with upward ascent. He was 2 years old when he discovered stars in the sky, and it was like a light went on in his mind," she said. "He was a kid you couldn't hold back."

She was amazed at what he could climb—daunting walls in Eldorado Canyon and the Black Canyon of the Gunnison. She said she loved to look at the photographs he brought back from climbing trips, but often told him that she worried about his safety.

"Mom, I've gotta live the life I'm gonna live," he would say.

She marveled at his physical strength. The little boy who used to collect rocks, bones and skulls on his hikes in the foothills near Conifer grew into a man whose long fingers were astonishingly strong. Hampson could find a hold on a rock flake that looked impossibly small and incapable of providing a place that would help him propel his lanky body up to another improbable-looking grip.

Hampson was 6'5" tall, towering over most of his climbing buddies. Generally, climbers are shorter than average, using their small size and light bodies to move in a way that seems to defy gravity. Hampson used his size to his advantage.

Partly for that reason, Hampson ignored what climbing guidebooks had to say about routes. Instead of reading up on predecessors' techniques, he liked to eye a prospective climb, looking for the line—the route—that he thought presented a challenging but manageable way to the top.

"He was more interested in the aesthetics of the line," Van Dam said. "He'd look at something, and find a line, and tell me, 'That's what we're climbing today.' I'm the one who'd go back and check the guidebook to see if there was a scary runout—a long stretch where a climber would be exposed to a big fall—or something. He led some of the scariest stuff I've had the privilege to follow."

Hampson was a natural athlete, a good mountain biker who liked to compete in the races near his home in Breckenridge. He also was a gifted snowboarder.

Last summer, he set up a tent and a permanent camp on a mountain near Breckenridge and lived there until winter began moving in. Even after he got a roof over his head, Hampson still dressed pretty much the same. In midwinter, flip-flops were his preferred footwear, and even on a viciously cold day, he rarely wore more than his standard shell over a tee shirt and jeans.

He worked part-time at Breckenridge Recreation Center's climbing wall, helping climbers practice their moves and working out a few moves on his own. He also worked as a bellman and driver at Beaver Run Resort and at the Regal Harvest Hotel in Boulder—jobs he saw not as careers but as financing for climbing trips.

Once, his mother talked to him about her concern that he might die before she did.

"Chris, you know, the parent's supposed to go first, not the kid," she told him.

"Mom," he replied, "when it's time for me to go, then I'm gonna go, and if it's tomorrow, then that's when it's gonna be. When my time is up, it's up, but I can't worry about that. It's not about how long I live. It's about living my life, and loving every moment, and getting as much out of it as I can."

Survivors include his parents, Carol Hampson and Alan Hampson, his stepmother, Susan Hampson, and a sister, Kate Hampson. All live in Denver.

The trees in the forests are the disciples of the mountains which are the gods. They allow us to walk among them because they know that our actions are meaningless. No matter how much good or harm we do, time will undo it. We can raze the forests and level the mountains and time will bring them back. We can spend our entire lives trying to do good for the world yet the balance of good and bad will remain the same. By helping in one area, we do harm in another even if we cannot see it. If you try to change the world, you might miss the things that are happening right around you. Instead, pay attention to yourself and your surroundings. You can change the world more with small things like a smile or a positive attitude. Follow the things you love and people will notice in the way you carry yourself and in your happiness.

From the notebook of Chris Hampson

FREEDOM TO FALL

1 THE FALL

I was nervous about that particular trip. In his time off from work, Chris traveled many places to rock climb. It was his passion. I was used to his going off into the wilderness for as long as a month. And while I understood the dangers of rock climbing, I knew he was a skilled, cautious climber. But that trip felt different.

Throughout that fall and winter I had noticed the glow in Chris. He was joyful, full of life, funny. He'd tell stories about his life as a bellman at a hotel in the Colorado ski town of Breckenridge. At moments he'd have me in stitches. At other moments, he seemed increasingly wise beyond his years, knowing at twenty-five what I'd worked a lifetime to understand.

In February I called to set a time for our next dinner together in Breckenridge. "Is it okay if I invite a friend?" he asked. "You'll like her." My interest perked up. A girlfriend? That was something new. Chris sounded smitten.

It was a night to remember, freezing cold and snowing. Chris sat between us at the Japanese restaurant with a gigantic smile smeared across his face. He was brimming with affection and positively radiant. As we left the restaurant, he grabbed the sides of my furry hood and said, "You look so cute!" It was an expression of unrestrained happiness. I was thrilled. Chris was in love.

That spring we saw each other a couple of times, but the fates seemed to keep us apart. Snowstorms hit hard. Chris came down with the flu.

In April my daughter, Kate, called. She was having a hard time in school, unable to concentrate, exhausted. "Something feels very wrong," she said. I flew out to San Francisco to be with her. One day as we walked down the street, these words ran through my mind: *It's just going to be you and me, Kate.* The thought came through and was gone.

When I returned home I called Chris, hoping to see him before he left on a spring climbing trip. I was too late. He was leaving the next morning.

Kate needed me again and I flew out, thankful to be with her in a time of difficulty. School ended, and Kate came home the first week of May. All that month my mind was on Kate. She was having trouble thinking and sleeping; she wasn't herself. Day after day we confronted the problems upsetting her life.

In the third week of May, a friend flew down from Idaho for a visit, our first reunion in five years. We chatted incessantly, bought flats of petunias and planted them in the garden.

On Sunday morning, May 23, before taking my friend to the airport, I suddenly remembered my son. *Oh, Chris—I must call him right now.* There was a sense of urgency.

I got his answering machine. "Chris, where are you? I miss you. Call me."

On Tuesday he called back. "Hi, Mom."

"Where are you, Chris?" I asked, feeling apprehensive, then brightening with hope that he might already be home.

"I'm in Yosemite, getting fruit at the grocery store," he answered. "I'm sorry I didn't call sooner. I can only use my cell phone so much."

"Chris, are you having fun? Are you with other people?"

"Oh, yes, I'm having a blast. There's a whole community of people here. I'm staying in Camp 4." His voice was full of vigor.

"When do you plan to come home, sweetie?"

"Plan? What would I do with a plan? I'll come home when I'm ready."

I laughed. It was so typical Chris. "When you get home we'll have a barbecue. I love you, Chris."

"I love you too, Mom."

On a beautiful Thursday afternoon the last week of May, I opened the screen door and stepped into the backyard. The yard looked lovely with its fresh green grass and newly planted flowers. I eyed the new charcoal grill, anticipating family gatherings in the sweet summer months ahead. As I stepped back towards the door, I turned to admire the scenery once again. For an instant life stood still. A haze hovered in the air. I had the distinct impression that something was about to happen.

Between 9:30 and 10:00 on Friday night I was relaxing in bed, when a sparkling golden light swept into my room, surrounding me in a Heavenly glow. I felt wrapped in an aura of protection, as if I'd been transported to a magical place, very safe and wonderful. The light felt like incredibly deep love, like God was right there with me—and I couldn't imagine why.

Saturday morning I took a walk. The golden light had mellowed, but I could still sense it. *God has given me an incredible gift,* I thought, and wondered what it meant. Kate and I spent the afternoon at a frame shop, framing some of her artwork. She complained of lack of energy and motivation. She didn't know what was happening and seemed to be holding on by the barest thread.

Saturday evening an old high school friend called. Though we spoke occasionally when I visited my mom, he had never called me at home in the thirty-five years since I had moved to Colorado. When he asked about my kids, I told him Chris was climbing in Yosemite. He said, "Doesn't that make you nervous?" "Yes," I replied. "But Chris is a good climber, and he is careful and meticulous by nature. I take comfort in that."

I went to bed with my mind on Kate. *There is something in the human spirit that can rise above adversity. There is something of the miraculous that can work with whatever comes up. I believe in Kate. I will help her find her way.*

At four o'clock Sunday morning the phone rang. Instead of answering, I rolled over and drifted back towards slumber. Minutes later the doorbell rang twice, followed by loud knocks.

Kate called from her bedroom. "Mom? What's going on?"

"I don't know, honey." I grabbed my robe, hurried downstairs, and looked through the peephole. Under the bright porch light stood two policemen and a woman in street clothes. I opened the door.

"Ms. Hampson? May we come in?" The woman followed me to the couch. The policemen stood just inside.

"Your son, Christopher?"

"Yes?"

"He's climbing in Yosemite National Park?"

"Yes."

"He had a rock climbing accident yesterday, and he is dead."

I felt a firm hand over my heart. Chris—protecting me, soothing me, cradling me with love.

Kate ran downstairs. We held each other and cried.

Chris felt the calling of his deeper home. But before he could go, he had to be ready. He had to get everything out of this life that was possible for him. And he had to give up attachment.

When Chris was growing up, he was attached to the house, the forest, family, friends, his belongings. When he was ten, we were on our way to Homestead Days at the museum when a motorist hit us from behind, sending us into a fence and totaling the car. Though I bought a new car, Chris wasn't happy. He wanted the old car, which had been a daily companion. During his first year of college I gave away his summer camp trunk. He had painted it turquoise and filled it with relics: firecrackers, Legos, broken prairie dog bones, stuffed animals, crumpled paper. When Chris came to visit, he noticed that the trunk was missing and asked about it. When I told him it was gone, tears welled in his eyes.

The college years brought change. One day he came in with a friend and wanted to know if I had things in my new house that belonged to him. I asked him if he meant the things he had when he was a little kid. He and his friend had a laugh over that one. Moms would be moms. "No," he said, between chuckles. "I'm talking about climbing equipment."

Chris was attached to this earthbound existence. He loved his tattered climbing books and the feel of his old flip-flops as he walked uncharted paths. But his true attachment was to the freedom beyond clouds.

Perhaps I knew. Perhaps I've always known. Perhaps Chris came to me, to us, for some special purpose. Perhaps I will spend a long time learning to understand. In my grief I cannot yet fathom it.

2 THE EAGLE FLIES

Alan had been at his team's soccer tournament in Albuquerque. A teammate had wakened him in the predawn with the news of his son's death and then had driven him to my house in Denver. When Alan walked through the door, he was the voice of reason. "Carol, Chris died doing what he loved."

Meanwhile my family, whom I had called minutes after receiving word, was flying in from different parts of the country. They all arrived at once: Sunday night the doorbell rang, and I opened the door to find them clustered together on the front doorstep.

That night with everyone in bed and the house dark, suddenly the wind kicked up. Kate was gazing out my bedroom window. "Chris is shaking the trees for me," she said.

On Monday afternoon Alan swung open the screen door and stepped outside to the patio. I followed him out.

"I feel Chris," I said. All at once he was there, a sparkling aura close to the ground, curled into a radiant smile. At the center was a knowing eye. It was all Chris, the very essence of his being. *My, what an old soul!*

I saw that everything was as it should be. He was joyous, whole, and beautiful. Death had not scarred him, far from it. He was in his element. *Look, Mom, at who I have become.* What I saw was the ancient core of wisdom and knowledge, a soul on intimate terms with the universe. He had learned his lessons well, shed all burdens. His joy was absolute. Chris was a free spirit.

From this side of life, that is what I saw. It was the same Chris I have always known, only more. I called Kate down from the balcony. While Kate, Alan, and I sat with hands interlocked, Chris wrapped around us in sweetness and love. He entered my being and spoke the words we needed to hear. He spoke of a golden cord connecting us with him. He said he would always be with us. He said we would make it through.

At some point I wearied. The vision faded. Kate and Alan remained on the patio, while I opened the screen door and went back to bed. The next day my friend Vanessa came with yet more flowers.

"The energy feels different today," she remarked.

I blurted out, "Chris is gone. He's gone; he's gone."

I reached my hands towards Heaven and cried. Vanessa stayed right with me, looking into my eyes. Her black eyes held me, pools of light.

Chris had said that last time we talked that he wasn't ready to come home yet from Yosemite. Now I know he had to take that step that led him to his death. He had to die first, and then he came home, for the last time.

But Chris has *gone* home. I had him for twenty-five years. That is a long time.

After Chris died I kept a journal, recording my experience, seeking insight and help every day. Often I wrote directly to Chris, certain that he could hear me.

June 2, 2003

To my dear son, Chris,
The golden cord that ties us together cannot be broken. Is there anything you want me to know? To find the strength to endure this? This is final. I will never see you again. But you have been comforting me since word came yesterday. Your spirit is so precious and gentle.

June 6, 2003

Part of my mourning is to learn to feel okay about missing you, to know that your physical presence will no longer be here, that you will no longer bend down to hug me and tell me that you love me. You are one of God's own. You are part of the light of the universe. You were taken away from me, but I never had you. You were my child, and I loved you with all my heart. I gave you everything I know how to give, so that you could grow your own wings.

You did not have a long life, darling, and that pains me. But you were not concerned with how long you lived. You were a shining presence, and your presence lives on.

Pain exists especially when we hold on, cling to someone. But we cannot have anyone else. We only have ourselves. You came to me after you died and showed me your essence and that is what I have—your essence—so free.

It will take me quite a while to absorb all of this. It is a gradual unfolding. I need to be fearless in my approach to pain, not run from it but allow it to come through.

June 15, 2003

I am so grief-stricken. Today I need to help myself think about things in a certain way. I don't want to be so consumed by grief when it hurts so much. I need to come back to the bigger picture, beyond my own personal trauma. I need to help myself get up out of myself.

I can't bear this any longer.

Okay. It's okay to get those feelings out.

The worst thing is that I want my son back. That is what is so devastating. And he isn't coming back. This is so much the hardest part to deal with.

I know all of this pain is the not letting go. You hold onto your child and that only brings despair. So you have to let go every day.

I need help in the letting go. And I am getting that help right now. It's not just me doing this alone. Someone is helping me with the pain and suffering. It is the suffering that I want help with.

Receiving help—I feel myself receiving help. Thank you. I don't know where it comes from. So I need to keep coming back to these words—to let go—and I feel the comfort of letting go. And I know that all is well. There is something other than my grief, a calm place, a place of light. It is love that comes to me and helps me.

> To love someone does not imply clinging. The
> highest form of love is letting go. Love is not cling-
> ing. Love is always about letting go.

When a child is born, you hold that bundle of precious-
ness to your heart, and every day thereafter you let go a little
more. When a child dies, you unfurl your hands and blow, for
the child, endowed with Spirit, is now truly free.

Through days of mourning the loss of Chris, I seek the
guidance to release him. Each act of unleashing is an act of
love. To encourage the freedom of our children is the greatest
gift we can give. It requires seeing them, not as we wish them
to be, but as they really are, and nurturing the heartbeat that
is them.

There is order and beauty in the universe. Our children de-
serve to pursue their freedom—to die even—when God calls.

While Alan was on his way to Denver from Albuquerque, he
saw a cloud take the shape of a seven-pointed star. Later in
the week, while sitting in his office typing out an obituary notice, his forefinger kept involuntarily hitting the star key. "Stop
it, Chris," he said. Even then his son sported playfully with him.
Alan ended the obituary saying: "His extraordinary spirit is
now free and soars as an eagle." He had a photograph of
Chris copied and inscribed with those words for guests at the
memorial. From the moment Chris died, that was Alan's understanding of his son.

Alan and his wife, Susan, held the memorial service outside their home in Golden, in the foothills west of Denver.
Greg Van Dam was the first to speak, after the priest. Greg

told a story that Chris had told on himself. It was a bitter cold night in January. Chris was walking home through the forest after a party wearing only a light jacket and tennis shoes. The cold was biting into his flesh, and he wondered how he would make it home. He came into a broad clearing and saw the full moon on one side. He looked to the other side and saw an enormous shadow cast across the snow—his shadow, engulfing the entire field. Chris began dancing, making shadow puppets in the moonlight as he bounded for home.

At that point in Greg's story, as people were laughing, a golden eagle came out of the east and flew directly over Greg's head, casting its shadow across the gathering of friends. It circled three times and then flew off to the south.

That morning, in the midst of community and rarified air, Greg spoke the words we needed to hear. He had been Chris's principal climbing partner. They had learned together, lived outdoors together, and put their lives in each others' hands. Greg said, "Abraham Maslow, the great humanist, once wrote, 'A musician must make his music, an artist must paint, and a poet must write, if he is to ultimately be at peace with himself.' And so, too, a climber must climb, an outdoorsman must be outdoors."

Greg told Alan a remarkable story. The first week of May, Greg and Chris had met in Canyonlands in Utah, before Chris went on to Yosemite. For several days they camped and climbed and then decided to do a big climb in the back of the area.

> This trip was entirely magical. I believe that at some deeper level, we knew it was the last time we

Chris climbing the route Spaceshot, Zion National Park, Utah, April 1998.
Photograph © Greg Van Dam, 2009.

would be together, and so we thoroughly enjoyed each other's company.

Chris had selected the climb—Moses, in Canyonlands National Park in Utah, near Moab. It's a gorgeous tower, a monolithic rock formation that looms above the valley carved out around it. The climb wasn't a well-known one that gets done too often, but it features pristine sandstone crack climbing.

The long drive to approach it deters most people from going back to it. We loaded my gear into Chris's Subaru Outback and headed out the dirt road that would take us there. The road alone was one of the most interesting drives I've ever done. It winds down, quite precariously, the side of the cliff that drops into the valley. You can see the remains of rolled cars hanging off the mountainside where unfortunate drivers were not so careful. The views were spectacular, revealing the true power of weather and time. This magnificent valley had been carved out by a small river that we were heading towards.

Upon reaching the bottom, we continued driving along a sandy road that paralleled the river, winding around bushes and boulders. As we rounded a curve, in the middle of the road looking right at us, was an enormous golden eagle.

Chris immediately stopped the car, and we both just stared at the giant creature, expecting to catch only a glimpse as it flew off. But it didn't move. Chris grabbed his camera and jumped out, balancing his excitement with grace so as to not scare it off. As he approached the eagle, it began *walking* up the hillside away from him. I commented from the car, "It must be injured; I can't believe it's not flying off!"

Chris stopped his pursuit, and the eagle stopped, turned around, and just looked at him. Chris continued to walk toward it, and it continued up the hillside. When Chris stopped, the eagle stopped. When he walked, it walked. Chris kept holding the camera to his eye but never could get a clear shot of it. Finally, he put the camera away, took one last look at the eagle, and came back to the car.

He got in, and we drove on, talking about what a cool bird we'd seen. Just as we rounded the next corner, the eagle appeared again, wings spread, flying about a hundred feet above the ground, crossing the road just in front of us. Then it flew away in the distance. We were both amazed that it could fly! What on earth was it doing walking around, luring Chris up the hillside after it?

After the memorial service, Alan began seeing golden eagles every day. In the morning he would see them flying out of the south. Eagles flew over the mailbox as he went for the morning newspaper. Once an eagle came so close that he heard the whir of wings before he saw it. Another day he saw nine eagles. Eagles glided above the car on outings. He and Susan were watching them circle above the Fourth of July festivities in Breckenridge, when two broke off to soar over the bike race in the mountains, which included several of Chris's friends—the same race Chris had participated in the year before.

In mid-July two friends, just back from Yosemite, drove Chris's Subaru into Alan's driveway. At daybreak the following morning, Alan and Susan emptied the car of Chris's belongings—tent, climbing gear, bedding, clothing, camera, rolls of film. For days afterwards the car sat in the driveway. Alan couldn't bear to drive it. Nor could he bear to part with it. He couldn't bear to sell the car that Chris had bought new three years before, the car that was organized down to every detail, like Chris himself, which had transported him on climbing ventures all over the American West and Canada, and had carried him to his final destination. Several days passed. When Alan finally climbed behind the wheel and took to the road, an eagle flew directly in front of the windshield.

On sixty-one days over four months, from the time of the memorial service through September, Alan saw eagles. Then they migrated south for the winter. Eagle sightings are not common along the foothills of the Front Range. Alan had seen them perhaps four times in the previous nine years.

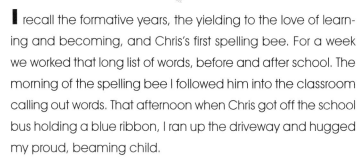

I recall the formative years, the yielding to the love of learning and becoming, and Chris's first spelling bee. For a week we worked that long list of words, before and after school. The morning of the spelling bee I followed him into the classroom calling out words. That afternoon when Chris got off the school bus holding a blue ribbon, I ran up the driveway and hugged my proud, beaming child.

I recall the butterfly print in spatters of green, red, and white that took "Best of Show," the replica of a space shuttle carved out of balsawood, the trombone and Colorado Honor Band, and the fund-raising drives when Chris took grand prize.

I know by heart that indefinable time between childhood and adolescence when a boy searches for purpose and refuses to be led. We would sit all afternoon while he twirled a pencil for the school paper due the next day. He made excuses at cleanup time. "Kate's not helping. Under her bed is a half-gallon carton of ice cream." Chris didn't have his heart in soccer, so I suggested martial arts. A friend knew of a wonderful school. The first day I planned to take him, but he walked off down the road. When I arrived in the car, he wouldn't get in. I told him he could walk the three miles home. He took his time, wandering the hills.

It was Chris's dad who helped turn him around. Every day Alan told Chris to get out there and run, even when Chris didn't want to run. Alan insisted that Chris earn his keep. He talked to him about passion. "Passion is the key to life. It is a reason to get up in the morning and the best reason to live." Alan wanted Chris to be passionate about something—anything.

When Chris was sixteen, he compiled a little book of inspirational poems which he illustrated and interpreted. It

Chris with Dad, after running with him to the top of the mesa.
Mesa Verde National Park, Colorado, June 1988.
Photograph © Alan Hampson, 2009.

included a picture of a young man climbing a mountain. Awaiting him at the pinnacle was a golden trophy. He dedicated the book to his dad.

When Chris discovered rock climbing, he discovered the instrument of change. The more he lived his passion, the deeper his experience and the more vital he became. "I taught Chris to run," Alan said, "and then I couldn't stop him."

Chris had a vision of enlightenment. But Chris simply *was* light. With his six-foot-five, two-hundred-pound frame, he walked lightly through the house. Light talk with Chris was good talk. He would race down the hill at lightning speed. He would jump to touch a beam of light. He tied knots with a light touch. He was lighthearted.

Chris moved through space with his eye on the big yellow ball in the sky. He became light as a feather. He became a bird who flies the way of the sun.

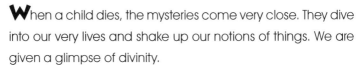

When a child dies, the mysteries come very close. They dive into our very lives and shake up our notions of things. We are given a glimpse of divinity.

Great Sky Spirit, may your days be filled with boundless joy.

3 MOTHER AND SON

How can I lose what never stood still for me?

Chris ran in and out of crowds, through fields of yellow grass, after tumbleweeds on a windy day. As soon as he was old enough, he set out in the world, disappearing and reappearing in our lives. He plowed up snowy slopes, vanished behind ridges, and reemerged on top, a towering, grinning bundle of delight. He careened down cloaks of cloud, wound up rivers of rock, wheeled with the whims of wind.

Sometimes we can spot him still—tumbling through the blue, carried on the gale, sweeping spheres of silvery mist, leaving behind a star-streaked trail.

How can I lose what never belonged to me?

Chris comes to me to tell me that the joy I saw in him will be my joy too. To believe opens life up in such an amazing way.

There are times, though, when all I feel is the loss of Chris. The pain is in my bones, and I am devastated. What then?

Everyone talks about what a good time Chris was having. I know that. But I also saw a different side to Chris. I saw him struggle at times.

The first time I visited Chris in college, we ate at The Sink, the iconic hamburger and beer tavern on the University of Colorado's famed Hill. Chris sat across from me. We didn't say much. He didn't look happy. My heart went out to him, but I didn't know what to say.

Chris was not always part of the in-crowd. He didn't hear well. He sometimes got sick. He wasn't naturally athletic until his later years, and there were some things he couldn't do well, like pull-ups. He didn't always feel understood. He felt lonely sometimes. He wasn't "up" every single day. He was sensitive. He was nostalgic. He could cry.

You don't love someone because they are strong. You may admire a person's strength, but you love someone because they are human. Sometimes when Chris and I were together—taking a long walk, sharing a meal—I would sense sadness between us. Neither of us ever mentioned it. It was as if we were hanging on to precious moments, which slip quietly away.

When Chris was three years old, at his annual checkup the doctor said, "He doesn't respond in the left ear." We went to a specialist. While plugging up Chris's right ear, the doctor sounded a loud buzz into the left. No response. He was profoundly deaf in that ear and had some hearing loss in the right ear at frequencies below speech. It was an inner ear disorder for which there was no remedy. We never learned when or why it happened.

When I told Chris he had no hearing in his left ear, he ran from me. That broke my heart.

Through the years I fretted inwardly about his handicap. He couldn't determine the direction of sound. "Where are you, Mom?" he'd ask when we talked from room to room. He was always swinging his head around, saying, "Huh?" He had to acclimatize to new voices. Whenever he had a cold, his hearing suffered. I worried about loud noises and his one good ear.

When Chris was nine, an otologist told him there was a good chance that in his lifetime he could get an operation to restore bilateral hearing, which would amount to sound being transferred from one ear to the other, where it would bounce off the inner ear bones like an echo. He patted Chris on the back and said, "You're going to make it, kiddo. You're going to be fine." But one day in his early twenties, out of the blue, Chris said, "Mom, my hearing loss doesn't interfere one bit with my quality of life. I am just as happy this way. I wouldn't get it fixed even if I could. I don't even think about it."

I know it wasn't always easy for him. He didn't like crowds. He positioned himself as best he could in a group of friends. He listened with his whole face. His golden eyes were extra alert.

The first time I visited him in Breckenridge, he showed me around the hotel where he worked as a bellman. On his locker there was a sign that read:

> Yes, I'm deaf…and I'm ignoring you.
> I hope this clears up any confusion.

A mother mourning for her child is a beautiful sight. It is a reflection of the deep love. Chris says,

> *It's okay, Mom, to shed tears for me. But do not be sorry for my death. How long one lives does not matter. It is how you live life that matters. You can keep embracing life day after day for as long as you can. But there is a kind of clinging in that. To truly surrender to life is to be willing to give it up at any time. You, Mom, helped set me free, with all the love you gave me. You helped me evolve on my own path. This is the gift you gave to me, and now I will give to you for the rest of your days on Earth. You will be blessed. You will find joy, and I will always be with you. You are not forgotten. Take the time to be in nature, for it is there that you will find me the most. It is there that I will be closest to you. Everything is as it should be. My joy will be your joy.*

When I have feelings about Chris not living out his life, and how sad I am about that, I need only to return to his spirit to see how very joyous he was. He was a samurai—my Chris, a samurai. Chris achieved something very great. I am so very happy for him. Of course he would share that with me, like the time he shared with me the blue ribbon for the spelling bee, which I helped him win. Of course he would come back after death and share with me what he had become.

July 14, 2003

I still can't believe Chris is gone. I want him back so much. The ache inside my body is terrible. I know it will work its way out, but I won't have Chris again. And I can't stay obsessed about him. I have to move on. I want to speak with Chris's friends, and I need to begin to do other things. I can't continue to nurse my wound full time.

The question this morning is whether or not I can ever feel happy again. It is really hard to take this, and even if I don't allow myself to think of Chris being dead, I feel an emptiness inside. The loss of a child really is not like anything else. Your heart aches so much. You want that child back so much.

To lose my own son, Chris. What am I to do? Chris can't come to me to comfort me. He was snatched away, never to be seen again. His body is gone, burned to ashes.

I don't like to be around others too much. Nothing makes me feel happy. I can't resolve anything because there is no way to get Chris back. He is gone. It is irrevocable.

It pains me to look around at Chris's pictures. And for all my explaining, it seems to me that he just accidentally slipped on a bit of rock.

How can I keep living without him? I don't want to. I want to die. To wake up every day and know that Chris isn't here—it is so very hard to accept. No more will Chris drive his car or climb a mountain or go to work. No more will he eat a meal or walk down the street. No more does my son exist.

It is good to get up and cry first thing in the morning. Regardless of how I want to interpret things, it doesn't matter. You can't hold on to interpretation. It isn't my place to keep evaluating the purpose behind Chris's death. All of that is like sand sifting through my fingers. I try to hold on to that and I can't. All I can do is accept that Chris has died. All I can do is take each moment and receive what comes to me. To receive my life, however it manifests.

I want to be able to feel happy again. I need to come back to myself, my own being, separate from all other beings because even though Chris came through me, he was not me, and his spirit is his own. Just keep coming back to myself.

July 18, 2003

Dear Chris,

Have I told you how much I love you? You are my one and only son, and I was blessed to have you. Now you have gone on, away from Earth. I do not know what has become of you, whether that energy has dissipated into nothingness or whether it has taken another form. Those are not questions for me to answer or even contemplate.

I mourn for you because you lost your life. But the golden light that came into my room the night before you died—there seemed to be a higher purpose. Why you were taken I cannot know, but it is as if it were all meant to be. . . .

July 20, 2003

Sometimes you have to be able to look truth in the eye and face it. Maybe the accident could have been avoided; maybe it wasn't God's will after all, but that Chris was not careful enough. Maybe it is exactly the way it looks, and I haven't been able to face those facts, shielding myself from them under a barrage of justification and explanation.

Either way I have to make my peace with it. Was I remiss in not talking to Chris about being more careful? No. Chris was a highly skilled climber. My mentioning it wouldn't have changed anything.

Perhaps Chris was responsible for that accident, and it wasn't God deciding to take him but that Chris did cause his own death—that he hadn't learned the lesson that you have to protect your life; it's not just left up to fate. I have to live with that and not be fooled into thinking that carelessness had nothing to do with it, live with it being an avoidable accident, that it wasn't predestined.

I must bring myself to a sense of peace about it, and not say "if only," but accept. Accept that there was nothing saying that Chris couldn't have had a long life, accept that his choices were fully his responsibility. Does God ever lead one to death intentionally? Or is death just the result of a person's actions, and nothing is determined before it happens?

Maybe the golden light was my own uncanny sensing of things. Maybe it wasn't God or Chris at all.

But I mustn't dwell. It will crush me. If the truth is that everyone is responsible for their own actions, that God is not causing us to act a certain way—if that is true, and accidents are what they seem, that someone playing with high stakes isn't paying attention—then I have to make my peace with that and let it go.

When I find myself saying, *if only this* or *if only that,* I engage in wishful thinking, wanting things to have a different outcome. I must come to terms with the facts. . . .

July 20, 2003, evening

I had been given the notion that Chris died on impact. Now I've learned that he was alive and moving after the fall. Chris's friend Tamara told me it was in the newspaper.

All those questions I had today about Christopher, and how he felt about losing his own life, when he hung there conscious and moving and knowing he was dying—my God. There are questions and doubts that torment me, but I will never know what he thought, the same way we can never possess someone else's thoughts, nor is it our place to try to do so.

Trust is so important—to allow trust that things are as they should be to take hold of me and have that inner discipline to maintain my peace of mind. There are many areas of doubt where the mind can dwell. But the discipline is to stay with trust and love, and that will be my salvation.

July 21, 2003

Last night, a reminder of Chris's presence, with all of his love and sweetness, surrounding us on the second day after death. A wonderful feeling, that Chris was such a loving spirit and he felt so very fine about where he was.

This can be a turning point in my grieving. That his love and sweetness will always be very close to me—a shift away from *imagining* Chris, into the energy of Chris.

July 24, 2003

. . . I think it best not to hide from your photographs. But it is sad to look at you physically, and to know that you no longer exist. Your precious body and your precious personality—all gone forever. Yes, it is so very difficult for a mother to come to terms with that, to look at your picture, to be reminded of you, when you are no longer on this planet.

To look all of this in the face is to have courage, to see you, dear son, in all of your stages of growing up, to see you and know how I have loved you with all my heart. But you are not here to receive my love any longer. And yet still, the love in my heart is full, and you will always be with me. . . .

August 1, 2003

I do have control over certain things, but I have no control over what happens in this world, what happens to my loved ones. I cannot ever evaluate the real meaning behind Chris's death. I can say that I help ensure my own longevity. And I can say that Chris was not ensuring his own longevity, and I can say that he should have been. Or I can say that his life cycle was complete, and he didn't need that. I can say there is only this life, or I can say that there is more life beyond—and depending on my answers I can then feel reassured or I can feel pain.

I must let go of all those attempts to explain. I have to accept that Chris was not holding onto life; he just wasn't. It isn't a should or a shouldn't. It is the simple truth.

I'm not ready to see all the facts of the accident. I don't want to know. It is better not to know.

August 4, 2003

My pain can be described as an estrangement. I am taken out of myself into an unfamiliar, unsettling realm where everything hurts. I have lost possession of myself. This estrangement is like a splintering. When someone dies there is estrangement not only from the self but from the world. And there is a constant thinking of the person, which is out of balance. . . .

My estrangement from the world is the attempt to stop the world, stop life because my son has stopped breathing. Babies are born, people laugh and dance and get what life they can. The generations go on—grandparents, parents, and children—while a dear one in my family is gone. I do not recognize other souls bustling about as if nothing is wrong. I only recognize my son, whom I have lost.

To be so absorbed, so out of step, to shield myself from life itself, to experience pain even in sunlight and mountains, sky and rainbows—*no!* Give up this absorption. The pain comes in the imagining—imagining that I will never see Chris again, imagining that he went out of existence, imagining events of the past, imagining that Chris will not grow old. All this imagining takes me out of the present moment. This moment holds no pain. This moment simply is. There is no pressing need here. This moment holds no grief at all, only stillness and lightness. . . .

I can say this is required of me, but that is a bit harsh. Instead, say this is the way. This is the path. One has only to be attentive. I must keep at it, bring myself to this every day. The universe has positioned itself differently. Everything has changed. It is all in learning to be attentive.

August 14, 2003

What are you supposed to do when your son dies, and you must go on living, when you see his smile, his sparkling eyes and his tall, handsome body wherever you look, when you hear his voice and ache for him in your heart? What are you supposed to do?

It seems that it is time to drop all pretenses. Speak the truth, and go out into the world knowing that this world is not complete, far from it. Be available to others and speak the truth. Do not pretend to be strong, for strength is false at a time like this. Do not keep up appearances. Rather allow my grieving to shine through, and accept the incompleteness of life.

The days are ending when I can afford to stay isolated within the confines of my own home. In some ways that only deepens my grief. Grieving is such an inward experience that it is easy to lose balance. Others help to bring me out into the world of sunshine where things are happening.

Know my son is missing, no longer among us, and yet I must go on. Know that life is exactly what it is. Judge it not good or bad, but be a witness to its ups and downs. Expect not good things or bad things. Just say, *So this is life.*

August 15, 2003

Today is about coming back to myself. I have allowed my mind to wander far afield, and now it is time to come back home and once again connect with Presence. This is the only way to live my life. It allows me to experience life moment to moment, and it frees me from the bonds of the past. When I allow my mind to wander all over the place, conjuring up all sorts of images of Chris, attempting to understand where he is, being shocked all over again by his passing, giving my mind free reign to play havoc with my emotions and my soul, then I have become a victim unto myself and there is no redemption, just more of the same, day after day. It is a kind of dying within life.

So, I say, wake up! Wake up to the beating of my own heart. Hear the birds, rejoice in the mountains, breathe fresh air. Be alive again, and rest assured that I will feel the presence of Chris rise up within me and we will be one—presence to presence.

Stop this clinging, this feeling of absence, Carol.

I relinquish thoughts that lead me astray. Experience my own breath. Feel the beauty of being, and all things will take care of themselves.

September 1, 2003

. . . To access such a deep layer of pain is good. By opening myself up to the totality of my experience of Chris, I take steps towards quickening the grieving process and move closer towards the day when I will feel whole again.

No matter how I feel, good or bad, it doesn't change reality outside me. I can only change myself by embracing the good feelings when they come and embracing the devastation as it comes. The constant of Chris's death remains, but my relationship to it changes, day by day, week by week.

Sadness is a necessary part of loss. Grieving must have its day. Do not stop the tears. Allow them to freely flow. Do not turn from pain when it comes. Be with it and honor it. It will pass.

Know that this lament is not suffering, any more than winter suffers the loss of barefoot days through soft green grass. Sun-kissed crystals dangle from trees, and the white earth glistens. Honor winter, and know that spring will come. Flowers will bloom and the heart will heal. We will live and even flourish.

I beam love to Chris, and he beams love to me. The cord that joined us in the womb has become the golden cord, stretching between Heaven and Earth.

When parents let go, children grow wings. Chris would call me on his trips to surprise me, for I never knew when he would leave or where he might be. The first time, he was a freshman in college. He said he was leaving for Utah to climb with friends. I told him he didn't ask my permission. He said, "Can

Chris with Mom, celebrating his graduation from college, May 2000.
Photograph © Julie Hamilton, 2009.

I go?" Laughing, I said, "I think you're going." As if I hadn't noticed that my son had a life of his own.

After Chris moved to Breckenridge, I'd drive up and take him out to dinner. When we met at his house, I'd walk in, and he would say, "Mom, take off your shoes. Say hello to the dog." Then we'd sit on his bed, and he would show me his photo album with his latest climbing pictures.

A couple of pictures made me gasp. "Chris, is that you suspended between two mountains?" and "You're sleeping inside that tent hanging off a cliff?"

One night, as we sipped wine and ate crab cakes in flickering candlelight, I said, "I don't want you to die before I do. You and Kate are my greatest loves. I don't know if I could live if you died."

Chris shrugged his shoulders and said, "I could be run over by a truck tomorrow." Then he told me how dedicated he was to living every day.

"But, Chris, you can have a quality life while protecting the length of your life."

He leaned towards me and gently said, "I know I don't know everything. When I'm fifty, I might think something entirely different."

During his last days, he told a climbing buddy he was grateful that I didn't try to stop him from climbing, even though he knew it frightened me.

Children are not ours to keep. They come through the night, light our days, and are gone. Some die following their dreams. Chris had his gaze on the stars. Deep down in my heart I knew he was going, and I never tried to stop him.

4 SPIRIT OF THE MOUNTAINS

When Chris was fifteen he entered a bike race. The race went up and down a long winding dirt path through the foothills of the Rockies. I saw Chris fall halfway down a slope. He got up and kept on going. When we met after the race, he seemed unfazed. It was all part of the game.

Chris got good at mountain bike racing, although I never knew. The only hint was when he told me one day that his place in a race had not been accurately recorded. He shrugged his shoulders and said, "My friends know how I can ride." And he'd ride every day, if he could.

Chris got good at rock climbing, although I never knew. I only knew climbing mountains did something for Chris beyond what I or anyone else could give.

There came a time when the Spirit coursed down through him as he sat calmly on top of the world. He told me about it one evening over dinner. There was a look in his eye and a tone in his voice. And I knew he would climb every day if he could.

In the beginning there were many days when I felt that Chris's life was cut short and he could have lived to do many more things—that even if it was true that his spirit was part of the hills and the sun and the stars, still he had this one life on Earth, and it was aborted by a tragic accident that could have been prevented. It was hard to hold on to spiritual understanding, because the fact of the accident was more tangible, more real in the concrete sense of things—that he didn't have to die young.

I wanted to understand why Chris climbed, what it gave to him, why it was the heart of his life. Why would he do something so risky that it could take him from us forever? Why—when he knew I loved him so, and even told him that I didn't know if I could survive if he died before I did?

In August I began corresponding with Greg Van Dam, Chris's climbing partner. In Greg, I found a real ally. Greg gave me so much, helping me understand my son; he was resolute that Chris had not died in vain. In turn, he was encouraged by my determination to find meaning and even joy within grieving. He was grieving too. He lost his best friend.

August 10, 2003

I spoke with Greg, and the conversation was very energizing. It reaffirmed my belief that there is order in the universe, and behind the accident there was no accident. That it was time for Chris to take his next step. Greg spoke of how radiant Chris was when he visited the Waldorf school where Greg teaches and how the kids were climbing all over him, how everyone noticed him, and how they all loved him. Greg was very affected by my saying that I knew I would not continue to suffer and that good things would come to me. He said that he saw where Chris got his bravery.

Greg is a godsend. I told him that it wasn't an accident that he and Chris met and became best friends.

I had been so forlorn, I'd lost sight of my earlier sense. Now I feel there was purpose in Chris's death after all. We have pieces of that and will never have the whole picture.

Some of Chris's friends are asking about me. I want to see some of them.

August 18, 2003

Dear Greg,

This has been an unbelievable journey for me, and difficult, but I am going on with my life, little by little. I know that in the long run it will help me to be involved.

I hope I didn't give you the impression that I was looking towards you to be a replacement for Chris. I very much experience you as your own person with a wonderful life to live. Your bond with Chris is an added dimension, and one that will serve you well, I am sure.

Your life interests me, and I will always celebrate whatever good comes your way. Keep me informed from time to time. Also, when you are climbing those mountains perhaps you can find a rock or two for me. Rocks are better symbols of Chris than pictures. Pictures are still hard. I would rather have pictures of the mountains.

The words "St. Christopher" kept coming to mind, though I knew nothing about the saint. I did some research and was amazed to learn that our Chris is very much like St. Christopher. According to the story, St. Christopher was a giant of a man who roamed the wilderness in search of adventure and a master to serve. He came upon a treacherous stream and remained there many days, carrying travelers on his strong shoulders to safety on the other side. One day it was the child Jesus whom he unknowingly carried across.

Remarkably, St. Christopher is the patron saint of travelers and protects against falling and sudden death. I have enclosed a St. Christopher medal.

September 6, 2003

Dear Carol,

I loved spending time with you before I left Colorado, and I found our conversation so rich. I hadn't the slightest impression that you would search for Chris in me and only appreciate that we can maintain a relationship to support and contribute to each other.

I will be on the lookout for special rocks for you. I brought Alan a really cool rock from the walls in the Black Canyon. My goal is to bring him a rock from every place that Chris and I climbed together—that could take a while!

While I often sharply feel the void in my life since Chris's death, I deeply feel that my life has become fuller because of all that he has given me, before he left us and after.

I have enclosed a quotation from *A Course in Miracles* for you. Thanks for the St. Christopher medal. I will treasure it. Like you, I feel strongly that Chris embodies his spirit. May goodness keep coming your way, and may you find the joy that exists in every single day.

Peace and love,
Greg

From *A Course in Miracles:*

I am always with you.
You were never separated from Me.
If ever you feel alone, confused, or in doubt,
be still, go home inside you.
I am there, your Peace, Light, and Joy,
who you really are, One with Me forever.
I will never leave you.

September 10, 2003

Dear Greg,

It gives me much comfort and joy to hear from you. I am delighted that things are going well. The same is true for Kate. Since she returned to school in San Francisco, I am amazed how good fortune seems to fall in her lap. After Chris died, I told her that even though she still had issues with him, he was watching over her now. And that seems to be true.

I understand more than I used to. I can't see the point of clinging to Chris. It does no good, only brings sorrow, and alienates me from his spirit. I have been making strides in letting go, even though

I still hurt. But the hurt is mingled with awareness of Chris's presence. I feel his energy and love and know that he is with me.

I love your phrase, "Chris left us." That is different from saying we lost him. It implies an active step on his part and does away with the notion that we are victims of a loss. Never again will I be afraid of death. We have an opportunity to go gracefully and beautifully to our deaths. Chris has led the way. That he was (is) my child is truly a gift.

Love,

Carol

September 20, 2003

Dear Greg,

Life goes on and I must go on. It is important for me to write every day so I can arrive all over again at an understanding of things. Eventually I think there will be greater acceptance so I don't have to work so hard. I can feel some rebound, but it goes slowly. Sometimes I think, *Oh, well, I'll make the most of what I have left. Perhaps someday I'll feel gladness again.* I know Chris does not put up with my brooding. He absolutely insists that I live a full life.

I speak with Alan some. Sometimes he can talk. Other times it is difficult. I know he is taking Chris's death hard, yet there are those eagles that help him enormously. Chris's spirit could be many things. Often I perceive a sprinkling of stardust when I am in bed. I have started thinking that Chris is also the wind and the brilliance of autumn. I feel a new chill in the air and think, *Oh, that's Chris.*

I am faced with having to reconcile what I think spiritually with the cold, hard facts. That is why

I must write every day. It is elusive, but I must stay the course to trust what I have gleaned. Insights come all the time. Most especially I must return to my own life and trust that this rawness will go away.

November 2, 2003

Hi, Carol,

Chris left us all with so much, from the beginnings of new journeys to new perspectives and ways of living. I still think how he helped elevate my own climbing level through the climbs he selected for us to do here in Sedona and in Moab—our last climbs together. They were of a different character than many previous routes.

I remember a conversation with him in Eldorado Canyon after I commented what a solid head he had and what a consistent climber he was. His response I still keep as one of my basic training philosophies. He told me that he simply loved climbing and did it for the pure joy of the act itself—*not* for ego reasons, to climb to a higher grade, to be known as a climber, or anything else that isn't real. He said that the reason his head was so together is because he logged so many miles on routes. While I spent time in the gym training and trying to get stronger, he spent time on the rock, moving over stone for the spiritual experience that comes from that—a calm mind and steadfastness.

It seems apparent that Chris covered many bases before he left. That was clearly exemplified in our relationship. I also think about how, not really being the relationship type, he finally managed to taste love and an intimate relationship within the

Greg Van Dam, on left, and Chris on top of Cathedral Peak, Yosemite National Park.
High school graduation trip, May 1996.
Photograph © Greg Van Dam, 2009.

year. And his beloved Yosemite was his obvious last stop! From the moment we rolled in there on our high school graduation road trip, he was in total reverence of the place.

I wonder how you are doing on a daily basis. How is your feeling life, your energy, your happiness? I think of you often, and Chris lives with me daily.

Love,
Greg

Dear Greg,

I did something very brave yesterday. I called the ranger, Lincoln Else, in Yosemite, who was one of two climbing rangers first on the scene. Until now I couldn't bring myself to face the accident.

Lincoln gave me a sketch of what he knew. Then I lay down a while as I felt quite shaky. But it was an important step. I also called Sibylle Hechtel, Chris's climbing partner that day, and left a message.

You ask how I am doing. I feel heartsick, but I try not to move into that space that is so painful. It is easy to feel good when I connect with the spirit of Chris. It is the physical loss that is still hard. But I am better than the first three months or so, when at times it was unbearable. It is bearable now. And I am aware that it is the thinking of things in a certain way that brings pain, not the actual death itself.

In the spring I'm going to Yosemite. It will be hard, but it is necessary. I need to feel the energy of the place, go to the base of the mountain Chris was climbing when he fell, go to Camp 4, talk to climbers, and maybe scatter his ashes.

November 14, 2003

Dear Greg,

There are things that come up in the course of speaking to Chris's friends that contradict what I prefer to think, and I feel very sad all over again. I have learned that Chris had plans after all. He wanted a family. He really wanted kids. He told friends how much he loved children. I'm realizing that Chris had more living to do.

But I still feel that underneath, his spirit was ready to make a big leap. Of course, Chris had aspirations, just like most people, but something much grander was at play. The soul is housed in the person, but it may be whistling a different tune.

It's just something for me to deal with. That Chris wanted a family . . .

November 15, 2003

Dear Carol,

I would like to share with you some excerpts from one of Chris's books that Alan passed on to me. It is called *Zen and Japanese Culture*, and Chris often referred to the philosophy in it during our conversations.

> Zen is discipline in enlightenment. Enlightenment means emancipation. And emancipation is no less than freedom. We talk very much these days about all kinds of freedom; political, economic, and otherwise, but these freedoms are not at all real. As long as they are on the plane of relativity, the freedoms or liberties we glibly talk about are far from being such. The real freedom is the outcome of enlightenment. When a man realizes this, in whatever situation he may find himself he is always free in his inner life, for that pursues its own line of action. Zen is the religion of *tzu-yu* (self-reliance) and *jizai* (self-being).

I bring this one up because I have no doubt that Chris's main goal in life was to attain this enlightenment. His avenue was primarily through climbing. This is not merely a belief of mine, but something Chris and I talked about in many different forms, which will make more sense with the next quote.

> As a Zen monastery is usually situated in the mountains, its members are in the most

intimate touch with nature, they are close and sympathetic students of it. They observe plants, birds, animals, rocks, rivers which people of the town would leave unnoticed. And their observation deeply reflects their philosophy, or better, their intuition. It is not that of a mere naturalist. It penetrates into the life itself of the objects that come under the monks' observation. Whatever they may paint of nature will inevitably be expressive of this intuition; the "spirit of the mountains" will be felt softly breathing in their works.

When I said at the memorial "a climber must climb, an outdoorsman must be outdoors," I was aware of Chris's membership in a spiritually elite community. He was incredibly aware of the "spirit of the mountains," and this intuition is obvious in his art form—that of dancing on rock.

Joseph Campbell (the world's foremost authority on mythology and comparative religion) speaks of the ultimate goal in our life as aligning ourselves with our bliss. If we are able to do so, we put ourselves in accord with a natural path that has been there all along. I think he is alluding to the greater scheme of things, the "momentum of the universe," if you will, the direction of the universal spirit, which is beyond our comprehension as human beings at present. Every human being has an innate bliss, and, given our karmic disposition in life, we live into it as best we can. Chris followed his bliss completely conscious of it on the physical plane. He responded to his bliss, and his life and death have paramount importance. I cannot begin to explain it, but I can feel this direction in my own life, and I think that any being so attuned can feel it and align themselves with their destiny.

Of course Chris spoke of the possibility of having a family, of having kids. But he lived his true path, the only one that could put him in accord with his bliss and the spirit that permeated his being.

Would Chris be disappointed that he didn't have the opportunity to experience this aspect of family? Not the Zen master that I knew. We had a conversation about regret once, and I shared with him a favorite quote of mine which he liked very much. "What is my religion? To live and die without regret" (Milarepa, Tibetan yogi/poet, 1052-1135).

Chris certainly had plans, and he lived them. This is difficult for many to understand, and if I had not shared life and death circumstances, the many adventures, senses of success, and full-on spiritual experiences in nature's greatest cathedrals with him, I would not understand it either.

May you keep the faith and a clear awareness of the Spirit.

Love,
Greg

December 27, 2003

Dear Greg,

I haven't told you yet about the miracle of Christmas. During the season Chris came close to Earth, and I could feel him watching over me like an angel. Everywhere, I encountered gifts of happenstance and the kindness of strangers. When church bells began chiming Emmanuel, piercing the cold city air, I could hear Chris in those bell tones, soothing my sorrow with glad tidings.

This year I bought everyone in my family a St. Christopher medal. For my mom I selected a beautiful nineteenth-century eighteen-karat gold one from

France. I also bought Florentine St. Christopher statues. Most special of all, I had Chris's writing, which Alan found in his notebook after he died, calligraphed and framed.

I decided to buy a live potted tree to celebrate the aliveness of Chris. I spotted it as soon as I walked in the nursery—a beautiful Australian pine. I took it home, wrapped the base in the Indian blanket Chris had given me, and put a gift for Kate underneath.

Last Christmas Chris had said, "Mom, from now on you only need to give me one gift—a climbing rope—one for every year. In response, I told him I would be happy with a cookbook every year. On Christmas morning he found a handsome multicolored rope under the tree, while I received from Chris the cookbook I had been coveting for weeks. This season I kept pulling it from the shelf, poring over the recipes, and holding it to my heart.

Two days before Christmas the mailman dropped a package from Cook's Illustrated Magazine through the mail slot. I thought, *Someone sent me a cookbook.* I put it under the tree and forgot about it.

When Christmas Eve arrived, I had the strange sensation that Chris was up to something. That evening a few close friends and family joined me for a candlelight meditation in Chris's honor, followed by a festive dinner. I could feel a sprightly aura, but nothing more. *It's just my imagination. It's time to get on with my life,* I urged.

On Christmas morning Kate and I opened our gifts. She gave me a beautiful handmade book of her own paintings and poetry.

"Look, Mom," Kate said. "There's one more package under the tree."

"Oh, I forgot. Someone sent me a cookbook." I opened it up and began flipping through the pages, exclaiming over the tempting recipes and illustrations. I searched for a name tag, but there was only an invoice, asking me to call with my payment. Kate and I laughed, wondering who sent it.

"I've never even heard of this cookbook," I said. Suddenly we looked at each other in surprise.

"Chris sent it!" I exclaimed. "This is the miracle of Christmas!"

Chris gave me one more precious cookbook, but I couldn't give him another rope. He climbs unbound. One day I'll join him. While he scales hallowed hills, I'll cast my cookbooks to the Earth's far corners and feast on Heaven's bounty.

Love,
Carol

P.S. As I told my Christmas story to others, I got blank stares. I couldn't make it out. Then it came to me. I realized that a miracle is a personal affair. It is between the sender and the receiver. To the outsider there doesn't seem to be anything out of the ordinary. What I suddenly understood is that a component of miracles is the ability of the receiver to recognize the miracle. It came to me like a bolt of lightning. It would mean nothing to someone standing on the outside.

January 2, 2004

Dear Carol,

First of all, Happy New Year! I want to refer back to your letters and address some of the subjects you were inquiring about.

I would like to start with a couple of quotes I came across in my climbing journal the other day. I was reading my notes on Monkeyfinger Wall, which is the first wall that Chris and I slept on with the portaledge*, in Zion. The first quote describes not only the mountain, but Chris as well.

> Mountains are quintessentially emblematic of abiding presence and stillness. . . In the fall, the mountain may display a coat of brilliant fire colors; in winter, a blanket of snow and ice. In any season, it may at times find itself enshrouded in clouds or fog, or pelted by freezing rain. The tourist who comes to visit may be disappointed if they can't see the mountain clearly, but it's all the same to the mountain—seen or unseen, in sun or clouds, broiling or frigid, it just sits—being itself.
>
> (Jon Kabat-Zinn, *Wherever You Go, There You Are*)

The second quote reminds me of Chris's wonderful sense of humor. He made this comment as we were sitting on the portaledge, in the darkness, eating power bars for dinner by headlamp. We were discussing women, and he concluded the conversation with a quote that he heard from Derek Hersey (a well-known climber who died free soloing). "Sure climbing can kill you, but women can destroy you!" We had a good laugh at that one.

In response to the miracle of Christmas, I refer again to one of my favorite texts, *A Course in Miracles*. It describes the principles of miracles.

> Miracles occur naturally as expressions of love. The real miracle is the love that inspires them. In this sense, everything that

* This and other climbing terms are defined in the Glossary, pp. 153–156.

comes from love is a miracle. . . . Miracles are natural. When they do not happen, something has gone wrong. . . . Miracles are healing because they address a lack; they are performed by those who have more for those who temporarily have less. . . . Miracles reawaken the awareness that the spirit, not the body, is the altar of truth. This is the recognition that leads to the healing power of the miracle.

I honor your receptivity to Chris's miracle and know that your recognition brings a great healing power with it.

Peace and Love,
Greg

January 10, 2004

Dear Carol,

Your last letter left me concerned as you mentioned the difficulties that come with the month of Chris's birth. I hope you are okay and that you continue to celebrate this month that brought him into the world.

You asked about meeting in Moab for Chris's birthday. It is very important for me to be climbing on the day of his birth as I believe it will resonate on some level with him. However, I have been checking the Moab forecast, and it looks grim. Joshua Tree is an option—the weather is beautiful this time of year. Let me know what you can manage. I would love to be with you on such a special day and even take you climbing if you want. It would give you a feel for what Chris was so passionate about.

5 THE FIRE OF LIFE

Nurturance is the bedrock that allows the soul to thrive. To nurture myself now is to be light with myself, joke with myself, laugh gently at my gravity. To nurture myself is to take care of my needs in the best way possible—to rest, take walks in the mountains, soothe this rawness, and become creative again.

To nurture myself I only need to receive whatever comes my way, accepting that life just goes on. Witness this life. See that it is but a single stop in the journey of the soul. Be in relationship with others.

There is no need to block experience. Don't hide from the things that cause pain, for they are tools for healing—sunlight, children playing, the patter of rain, the smell of pine. Receive fully my life this moment, and I will be carried forth. Lay bare my wound and allow it to bleed. Go forward with the sense that things are as they should be, and my loss will be transformed.

In September that first year, I returned to work with a dinner-performance of "The Hobbit" at the Vanilla Factory Coffee House in Denver. Before Chris died, I had been staging events there on a regular basis. The shows combined my two loves, cooking and storytelling. I would cook and serve a four-course meal for about twenty-five people, then I would perform a story; the meal and the performance would be around a theme.

"The Hobbit" was the last story Chris had seen me perform, in the spring. He had arrived at my house feeling sick and wasn't sure he could make it to the show. While he lay on the couch, I rolled out a counter's length of dough for the chicken pot pie I would be serving. From the kitchen I could hear him on the phone talking to friends in Breckenridge. He talked fast and ardently. I could feel his urgency and his love. *My goodness*, I thought. *Chris doesn't lose a second of living. Even when he is sick, he carries on in the most heartfelt way.* I was aware in that moment of the rich bond he had with others. It made me tingle with happiness for him.

"I'll try to come," he said, as I left the house. He did come and was seated at a table with three strangers. Afterwards, those people told me that while the dinner was delicious and the performance captivating, it was Chris who carried the night. He had entertained them with climbing stories and had won their hearts. Others told me how impressed they felt in meeting him for a few minutes—his glowing vibrancy reached across in a handshake and a smile.

The Hobbit is Chris's story. It's all about him—the story of an ordinary being who dares to step beyond convention to live life at the level of its pulse. Chris didn't stay to hear the ending that night, but I tell him now, the way I used to tell my children fairy tales just before bedtime when they were young.

It was a May day when Bilbo Baggins came to the top of a rise and saw in the distance his very own hill. But he was a much different hobbit from the one who had started out on his adventure long ago. . . .

. . .This tale ends happily as all good tales should, especially tales of extraordinarily brave hobbits who go to the edge to live life to the fullest. Yet Bilbo never thought of himself in any grand way. One evening some years later when he was writing his memoirs he stopped and reflected, "Concerning dragons and kingdoms, perhaps it is true that I played a hand in helping the ancient prophecies come true, but I am after all only quite a small fellow in the big wide world, and thank goodness for that."

I saw Chris a couple more times after that performance. In May he died. Before my first venturing forth after that, my performance at the Vanilla Factory, I was thinking about the line, "It was a *May* day..." *I will say it,* I told myself. *I will give voice to the month of May.*

When I called Craig Hospital to find out about volunteering, the only position available, amazingly, was in the cooking class.

Craig is one of the best rehabilitation hospitals in the country for patients ages fifteen to thirty-five with spinal cord or brain injury due to accident. Eighty percent of the patients are male. I began without quite knowing what led me there, but it felt right, and it gave me some interaction with folks who were struggling with a whole new life.

I thought about Chris ending up at Craig and am glad that he was spared a life of serious disability. But from the perspective of the hospital, life is important no matter what. I have thought that perhaps when the soul has good reason to cling to life, it will. Otherwise it is set free to travel new dimensions.

In cooking class I helped the occupational therapist. Patients practice sequencing, using utensils, staying on task, working as a team—real-life skills. I saw their faces light up when they cracked eggs into a bowl, opened a package of cheese, cut an onion, or served as team leader. When we sat down to eat, we were like a family.

I am impressed with the upbeat atmosphere at Craig and the caring quality of staff. The patients often are still undergoing operations. Many are in pain. All are adjusting to a major permanent life change. Some talk about their accidents and the first grueling weeks afterwards. I saw how far many had come in acceptance and determination. They were not focusing on the past but on daily challenges. I saw them taking pride in progress, however small each step along the way.

I also saw the anxiety some felt when it was time to leave. Others seemed happy to be moving on. Most go home to loving families, whose lives have also been changed, but who are so thankful to have their loved one back.

Every instant is a possibility, every second a potential, until I respond. Wherever I step, potential becomes reality, the substance of my life.

I can live for yesterday and tomorrow, and that will be my fate. I can release the past without grasping for the future, and that will be my fate. Either way it is a life of my own choosing. I can keep to the path of familiarity, leading nowhere, or I can step to the brink, overlooking the abyss.

How can I choose to live with no knowledge of where I'm headed? What anchors me if not my memories and expectations? I listen. *Step this way, now that,* trusting the voice within. Leaving behind old themes, I begin to slip into sync.

To follow fate is to recognize that you cannot direct your life. No matter how hard you try, life eludes. You can stop where you are, settling in, or you can keep going, listening and stepping. You have to be willing. You have to be strong and brave. You can't afford to lose another moment. To strive is meaningless. It is rather the absence of striving and the simple act of living that way.

Life is not waiting for me to get over my hurt. The universe conducts itself with forward momentum. I envy the flowers awakening, climbing, unfolding, and dying with singleness of purpose, day after blessed day. The height of perfection is but a moment before decline. The idea of loss denies the rhythm of life. Loss is an illusion, a reflection of the heart's desire.

O Mighty Wind, free me from the clutches of idle dreams. Let me be a wayward leaf, a wolf wail echoing down the canyon, a thousand crystals of falling snow. Pick me up by your talons and dangle me threadbare like a rag doll. Then toss me over fallow fields, so that I may rise among the clamor of blackbirds to feast on my own strewn seeds. Wind whispers, *Take hold of my sails.*

I had the sense of throwing myself away, directly into the fire of life. Since life had not come to me, I would go to life. I wanted to free myself and live life for the heck of it.

For a while I had been dreaming of cooking for the poor. One day I made a fluffy cloud of chocolate cake, cut it into pieces, got in the car, and began searching for some homeless people. Some folks were standing in front of the "Jesus Saves" shelter in downtown Denver not far from my house. A group came over as soon as I parked across the street. I handed over the cake. "Thanks, honey." "Are you coming again tomorrow?" "I'm hungry. This is really good cake!" It was my happiest moment since Chris died.

A few days later I took meatloaf and potatoes. Then I made loaves of pumpkin bread and took them hot from the oven in a snowstorm. The problem was that I would just hand the food over and leave. Many of them didn't even notice where the food came from. It just appears, and while they dive in, I drive away. I wanted more interaction. Next time, I decided, I would get out of the car and serve folks one at a time. That way I could see their faces and exchange words.

To cast myself away, walk out on a limb, and see what happens. That is my new take on life.

I sought out Chris's friends, traveling to towns in Colorado and occasionally other states to collect stories about Chris. I hadn't known many of his friends before the accident. I found names and phone numbers in the guestbook from the memorial service. One person led me to another.

Chris hadn't talked to me often about his personal life. We exchanged ideas, laughed about the simplest things, and enjoyed each other's company. But there was a lot I never knew about, like some of his ski adventures in the backcountry. I did know that he was knowledgeable about the backcountry and wore a helmet and avalanche radar gun his dad had given him.

I went to Breckenridge often. Several of Chris's friends there were bellmen at Beaver Run Resort, as he had been.

"My favorite memory," Scott told me, "was when Chris and I were chasing each other on snowboards during a snowstorm in thigh-high powder. Why go down the middle of the ski run when you can veer off to the left and then explore what's there on the right? No one else ventured towards the trail we were making. No one else had thought about skiing that way—your own line, your own path."

"We're jumping off cliffs," Kirk said one night when a group of us went out to dinner. "Chris looked at it like, *All right, I'm going to go off.* But he always had respect for the air he was about to take. There were a couple times when I saw that guy cartwheel from head to toe, completely stretched out before he ever hit the snow. Then he lands and takes the fall. Chris knew how to fall. He knew what life was, and he knew the risk he was taking."

"Remember the avalanche?" Steve said. "He was skiing wicked that day. It was a slow-moving slide, thirty feet across; he came down through it."

Chris Pappas, top manager at Beaver Run, told me that he was fascinated with Chris's rock climbing. One day in the fall he asked Chris to pick up a rock for him the next time he was on a mountain somewhere. They worked through the ski season and part of the summer, and Chris left on a climbing trip. When he returned, he walked into Chris Pappas's office with a huge grin, and without saying anything showed him a rock, then went to the computer and brought up a picture of the massive mountain it had come from.

"I had made that comment in passing," Chris Pappas said. "The whole ski season had come and gone, and he remembered. It's a small example of the kind of things Chris would do and how he thought. It made him happy to make other people happy."

Though it meant the world to me to meet with Chris's friends and collect their stories, it was often bittersweet; I would feel his absence. I felt as if I wanted to recapture him, when I could only get a glimpse through someone else's heart. It was a long time before I understood the gems I was garnering. Through the hearts of others, Chris came to life in ways I could not have known him otherwise, enriching my own memories. "He was a ray of light," Mrs. Goody, the widow of Chris's beloved martial arts teacher, told me, and I came to see that light penetrating every tale.

Eddie, a friend from the martial arts school, said the only way he could beat Chris sparring was to get him laughing.

Mr. Goody taught them to throw and fall. "It's a big accomplishment to get thrown for the first time," Eddie said. "The first time you're scared. Mr. Goody would say, 'Come with me. I'm going to help you take the fall.' It was like a dance. He'd move this way and that, and then there you were. You'd fall gracefully.

"We'd throw each other pretty hard. We'd get up and say, 'Let's do it again.' With Chris I'd think, *Let me handle this intellectually.* I'd try to get him laughing. Once he started, he was like a big teddy bear. He'd keep laughing. I'd say, 'That's the only way I can get you, man.' I still have the impression of him laughing all over the place and his big smile."

Eddie imagines that when Chris arrived in Heaven, Mr. Goody asked God to be allowed to go to Chris. He gave Chris a big hug; then he razzed him. He said, *All these years I've been teaching you to how to fall, and here you fell and couldn't even get back up.* And he imagines Chris laughing all over himself.

I wrote the stories down and passed them around.

Dear Mom,
I journeyed far. It was time to go. I could have eaten more mouthfuls of your poppy seed cake and chicken enchiladas, and relished more shared times and more ways for you to be a mother. But I lived as I was meant to live, and died the same. These realms are beyond imagining. Mom, the souls with whom I go cavorting would please you no end. But do not hurry here.

Your time belongs to Earth. You have more to live, more to learn, and more to give. Life snags you at every turn. Like rearing a child, it goes fast. I love you, and I am with you always.

The next time I went to the homeless shelter, I set up a card table on the sidewalk and served homemade shepherd's pie and salad to about fifty people. Such downtrodden faces! Some made eye contact and talked, while others looked down and quietly walked off to eat alone.

"This is really something," someone said. "I can't believe you did this, cooked it and brought it here, and set up this table, all by yourself."

"Aren't you afraid?" another person asked. When I said that I didn't see anything to be afraid of, he said, "I know there is nothing to fear, but most people don't know that."

"You are one of Heaven's angels," said another.

Two more people showed up. I scraped up the juices and tidbits from the bottom of the pans and handed over one last bowl.

"I'm sorry. I wish I had more," I said to the man who went without.

"Oh, that's all right," he said with a big smile. "You had to run out sometime. What you did was wonderful." Then he helped me get everything back into the car.

It was better than I had hoped for. To be up close, see faces, and communicate. I was elated.

The following week at the shelter, as I walked to the rear of my car to get out the pots of steaming hot chili and corn-bread, a man watched impassively, and our eyes briefly met. When I brought out the food, his face lit up. He helped me set up, then stood close by, supervising while I served the others. A circle formed around me, like old friends eating and chatting at an afternoon party. One man with a mischievous grin, cornbread stuck between his teeth, admitted that he ate three pieces. Others said to me, "God bless you," and, "You be careful."

It was a simple thing. I had taken delight in feeding family and friends, and it was only a matter of a few city blocks to go out now to feed those with whom I shared a raw vulnerability, where every word and look exchanged was nourishment for my soul.

New possibilities were appearing on the horizon—the idea that in losing my child, I could reach out in new ways. By putting one foot in front of the other, I was stumbling onto the discovery that with Chris gone, it was possible to go out there and live, with nothing to lose and everything to gain.

While still grieving, it is essential to keep moving. Moving comes through listening. I hear that I must not cling, for what once served me is already a ghost, only serving pain.

It is time to break the exclusivity of the mother-son relationship. It is time to explore and have some fun. It is time to take bold, new steps. And though the letting go hurts a little, I am willing to obey. It's time to run through wintry wind, share stories around the fire, embrace my hopes and dreams, and work ahead, for truly we are one, and we are each alone.

Each day some uncertainty asks to be explored, for the sake of truth. It is what I need to know in this moment, arising from circumstance.

The day came when, in the face of the ever-present question, I decided to respond: *I have a daughter. Her name is Kate.*

It was a long time in coming. My first opportunity to try it on came in a parking lot, speaking with a friend of my mother's.

"Do you have children?" she asked.

"I have one. I have a daughter. Her name is Kate."

Then I hesitated. I felt perplexed. It didn't sound right. It wasn't the truth.

She said, "Oh, it's a lot to raise one child, I know."

Though Chris now be a bird, I smile deeply into the adorable child that he was. For all things come to pass, and all things shall be, and never do we lose a single thing worth keeping. It is my truth, at this moment in time.

I sense that my life is about to change. Someone is tossing a ball in a snowy field. Someone is running to catch it. It is me.

6 LOVE OF CLIMBING

The September after Chris's fall, Alan organized the Chris Hampson Memorial Bike Ride in Breckenridge. After the ride, as everyone gathered on the terrace of Beaver Run Resort, I met someone who hadn't been at the memorial service. He introduced himself as Teague Holmes, saying that the reason he wasn't there was because he was still in Yosemite. Here was someone who had been with Chris! It was startling, a turn of good fortune, that I might learn something of Chris's final days.

Shortly after the memorial bike ride, I drove up to Breckenridge to interview Teague. He said that he hadn't known Chris well before Yosemite, but listening to him talk, you would have thought he had known him all his life.

Chris hadn't gone to Yosemite with a plan, Teague told me. Yosemite is huge—a climbing mecca with a big reputation—and climbers typically know what they want to accomplish. But Chris just wanted to climb, Teague said. "I was

Chris climbing Devil's Tower National Monument, Wyoming.
Photograph © Chris Hampson, 2009.

beginning to see just how much Chris loved climbing and being with people, because he was always up for anything. He was especially interested in routes that were adventurous and less well-known, routes he didn't know anything about except for what was written in the guidebook."

One such obscure route was called Demon's Delight. The approach to the route was a difficult, rocky, uneven gully, and Chris was wearing flip-flops, not the usual sturdy approach shoes. "I'm comfortable hiking on that kind of terrain, so I was wondering why I couldn't keep up with him. He was just flying up the hill in flip-flops! I got to the base of the climb, and Chris already had his climbing shoes on and had the route figured out. Oh, and another thing; Chris wouldn't care if he was leading or following. Most climbers want to lead the routes that will challenge them. But Chris was just happy to be out there climbing with you."

Teague led the first pitch, set up an anchor, and belayed* Chris up. He handed over the rack of gear and Chris led out, crack climbing horizontally under a roof. "I was watching him jam this thing out, wedging his hands into a tight-fitting crack. He disappeared around the corner, where I could hear him having fun. He was whooping, 'Heehaw,' and 'Oh boy, you're going to like *this* section!' which means, *This is really hard. Get ready.* There is a series of lieback flakes protruding from the wall. You have to lean away from the wall and climb hand over hand up the series of flakes. It takes lots of endurance. You have to hang in there and go for it, keep pushing through. Chris was placing gear all along the way because it was difficult. He made it through without falling."

* See Glossary, pp. 153–156.

On the fourth and final pitch, Teague took the lead. He came to one move, by which a climber mantles (steps) up onto a high shelf, and he couldn't figure out what to do with his body to make it work. He tried five or six times, then came back down. Chris said he would give it a try.

"When Chris got up to that point, he couldn't figure it out either. He came down, climbed up again, tried all sorts of things, then came back down. He climbed up and went for this one move, kind of desperate. He half fell, lowered himself, and he was looking at me. Finally he said, 'I'm going to try one more time. I've got an idea.'

"He climbed up there. His left foot was on a tiny rock crystal. His right foot was in this shallow toe jam. His right hand reached palm down on the shelf we were trying to mantle up onto; his left hand reached *way* up to a tiny, tiny hold that was worthless in my opinion. His 6'5" body was completely starred and stretched out, and his left arm was just wavering. I was thinking, *I'm belaying him, and he is going to fall and land right on top of me!* I was terrified. Suddenly he let out a scream; he caught that teeny hold and pulled himself up to the shelf, and he was freaking out. He was yelling 'Yahoooo' and making all these bird noises. To this day it was the purest form of joy I have ever seen. It was unbelievable! He said, 'That is the craziest move I've ever done on lead, ever!' He was exploding with joy.

"The funny thing is, I had to follow this. Chris had anchored the rope above me and was belaying from that position. I could fall all I wanted, and the rope would catch me. I climbed up and put my left foot on the little crystal and my right foot in that toe jam and thought, *You're kidding me.* I put my right hand down on the shelf, and that tiny hold he reached up to with his left hand looked like it was a mile up the valley. There was no chance of making the move. All at once I looked around the corner and saw a handhold that neither one of us had seen. I grabbed that, and Chris was yelling, 'What are you doing?! You're cheating!' Then I was stabilized. I stood up and made the move.

"So there was a hold that we hadn't seen. I think Chris was happy that he didn't see it. Some people would have felt disappointed in themselves for missing the hold, but Chris was saying, 'That's crazy! We didn't even see that!' He was psyched about it because of what he got to experience there."

Chris and Teague agreed to climb the North Ridge and Final Exam, adjacent routes on Half Dome. The North Ridge would entail a full-day ascent to the summit, so they decided to camp at the base of the routes, two thousand feet above the valley floor.

They headed up the six-mile trail carrying heavy packs and climbed Final Exam before dark, a single-pitch, 160-foot-long fist crack. "You fist jam when the crack is too wide to hand jam. We brought just enough gear, but Chris still had to run it out from piece to piece and climb bold. It was safe but scary, because the further you get away from your gear, the more intimidated you can be. Chris kept it together, real strong mentally. He kept going and making his moves. There were deep cracks where you had to reach in with your whole arm and make awkward moves. I slipped part way up and fell. Chris was up above, and he caught me and encouraged me."

Chris crack climbing Final Exam, Yosemite National Park, May 2003.
Photograph © Chris Hampson, 2009.

The next day they climbed the North Ridge, swapping leads. "We each shared the difficulties on that route, and we were each faced with different challenges. Climbing through those challenges, Chris just kept going up. Nothing could stop him. He climbed bold and solid, knew where he was and knew he could push through. It was eye-opening and inspiring to watch him, and that gave me confidence to push through my pitches as well.

"We got to the crux pitch, which thankfully Chris took because I would have been terrified. He climbed up and around the corner, out on the edge of Half Dome, almost four thousand feet above the valley floor. And that's a sheer drop down to the ground! It's the most amazing place. You're roped in, and you can take comfort in that and just enjoy the view. You are on this arête, with the rock going away from you in one direction and another, like the edge of a house, but sharper. Chris is out on the arête, looking up, saying, 'How could the route go *this* way?' The topo only tells you so much. It seemed improbable because there were no cracks where he could wedge in a piece of protection. But it appeared to be the only alternative, so he just kept going, trusting it would work out. I would have been hesitating a lot more.

"He came out around the corner, and sure enough there was a bolt right where it needed to be. So he clipped the bolt and then had to make this wild move from the edge of the arête. He had his feet up, and he was using opposing forces to push with his feet and pull with his hands and reaching way up into this crack, and again this is thousands of feet above the ground. It was so exciting to be in that position and watch him pull this off without falling. He went up and around, and he was having a blast. He was having an amazing time.

"I led the next pitch, which was an exciting, hard pitch, and he followed up. He was so good with recognizing what was going on in that situation. I just climbed a pitch that was a big accomplishment for me, and I felt great. He had a way of being plainspoken and real, without acting like it was a big deal, just saying, 'That was a nice job. That was an exceptional pitch and it took a lot to get through.' It was awesome to be with someone who could give a true recognition of what you were both experiencing and to connect and work together as a team. We topped out on the top of Half Dome.

"On the hike back down to the valley, we moved through the Death Slabs— treacherous, off-trail terrain, and plain and simple, I couldn't keep up with him. I would stop every once in a while and watch him, and he was just moving over this terrain so quickly. It didn't look like he was going very fast. He was just moving down the hill. And then there was my world—trying to go, sliding, and trying to keep up, and I thought, *If I keep trying to keep up with him I'm going to hurt myself.* Then I'd stop and watch him floating down through the trail and then back to my world, striving for balance and struggling to keep up. He stopped and waited here and there for me, and finally we started walking together at a slower pace.

"I said, 'Chris, I can't keep up with you. It doesn't look like you are going that fast, but you are just flying down the hill.' He laughed. 'My friends always give me a hard time about that. I don't know; I'm walking. I've been walking on this kind of terrain for a long time.' I asked him how long he had been climbing. He said, 'I started climbing when I was fourteen, and it is the best thing that ever happened to me. When I learned to climb I always knew.' 'What?' I asked him. 'Always knew what?' He said, 'I always knew what I was going to do. I was going to climb and keep on climbing until the day I die or can't any more. It was the most comforting thing to know that's what I love, and that's what I'm going to do.'

"I paused to take that in. Then gravity started having a way with him again, and the next thing you know he was a hundred yards away from me.

"That night I thought about what he had said. I love climbing, but not like Chris. Chris's priority with his life was spending time moving in the mountains, whether that was rock climbing, or hiking, or mountain biking. He spent his time and his priorities in motion, in the mountains.

"To be so comfortable with that, just to be so at peace with and aligned with what he loved to do, and to live it so purely. In contrast, I love all those things, but I'm always trying to do something better. I'm never quite satisfied with those things, even though I gain great benefits from them. But at that moment, when he told me that, I understood how he could challenge himself, strive for new climbs, and seek new adventure, but at the same time be comfortable and happy with where he was. That is a hard thing for anyone to balance. To have that hunger for different routes and more difficult routes, but at the same time retain that contentment with where you are right now. He had that. I became aware of how he was, and how it transferred to my life and could help me learn a lot more about myself."

7 TRUE FREEDOM

When your child dies, you learn to endure the depths, grasping for ground, rising and falling in an unfamiliar world. But how do I endure? Chris said, *I will be with you always. You can reach me at any time.*

Often I slip into longing, crushed by loss. Chris is nowhere. I am alone in my misery. The sacrifice is too great to bear.

Enduring is believing. When I embrace the spirit that is Chris, I find him everywhere. When I cling to the person he no longer is, I cannot find him. Every day I bring myself back to this awareness. If I am consumed by doubt, there will be doubt. If I am consumed by loss, there will be loss.

Enduring takes commitment and focus. It is daily practice.

I needed to have a plan for that first birthday. Christmas had come with its miracle, but his birthday loomed ahead. This seemed harder and more personal. How would I get through it? I couldn't just languish at home; it would be better to go somewhere.

I decided to go to Chris's world with Greg to celebrate him in nature—to Joshua Tree.

That trip was invaluable. I learned that miracles don't come when you expect them to, nor in the way you expect. I learned that God and Chris weren't going to save me from the pain of going through the first birthday. I was willing to go out into Chris's world and risk what that would mean—that I wouldn't find him there. It was something I had to learn.

January 17, 2004

Today is Chris's birthday. I am sitting on a boulder in Joshua Tree National Park of southern California watching Greg climb with his girlfriend, Sarah. With so many things going wrong—stalled traffic driving west, no vacant camping sites close to the climbing walls, Greg's car going dead—I'm getting the message that Chris does not want me to climb. He knows I'd be terrified! He doesn't feel that climbing is something for his mom to be doing. I'm relieved that I don't have to. I don't really want to. I'll be camp cook instead.

The scene here is stark: granite monoliths rising out of a sandy plain studded with the twisted, spiked Joshua trees, resembling shrunken palms.

Twenty-six years ago Chris was born. *Chris, darling, you came through me at 1:38. At the moment of your birth, the universe came into a certain alignment.*

Ten after one. The energies are quickening. I feel immersed in sun, wind, and rock. More climbers are starting up. *Though the route remains the same, the ascent is always new—uncertain, shifting and unfolding . . . .*

One twenty-eight. I am waiting for a sign. I yell up to Greg and Sarah, "In ten minutes Chris was born!" They say, "Oh." It is a tense moment on the wall. Sarah, a newcomer to climbing, is frightened. She can't find a hold. Greg is standing on the ledge above, encouraging her. They can't hear each other because of the overhang. I yell their messages back and forth, thinking Chris will help her up. She will step onto the ledge at 1:38—that will be the sign!

The wind and cold are fierce. More yelling as Sarah lifts, descends, pulls, gropes, and hugs the immense, unyielding rock. I am mesmerized, waiting for the next words to shout. I'm part of the team. I glance at my watch. One forty-five. Sarah is not going up, not this time.

I meander a long sandy trail, then go back to the car and weep.

January 18, 2004

So much for expectation. A voice whispers, *Destiny is not a given, rather a possibility. We mint our lives moment to moment.*

It was hard, this first birthday. I felt his absence. Today I am not looking for Chris, and I feel him again. *Mom, I am with you always.* Seated comfortably in a nook of warm rock, in the ancient refuge of high desert, pen in hand, insights come.

The universe needs the energy of enlightened souls. Chris gave up his attachments for a higher Truth. He loved all earthly things and beings, and still he let go. That was the great achievement of his life.

Saturday night I cooked turkey stew on Greg's camp stove. After dinner, as we kept warm by the fire, I asked Greg if he would be willing to talk a little more about his climbing partnership with Chris.

"Chris brought out a character trait in me that would not have been as strongly exhibited without him. He was really so passionate in climbing and adventure. He made me more intense and more extreme.

"I still remember him at Geneva Glen summer camp when we were fourteen. We were both interested in rock climbing, and complete novices. One day he suggested we sneak off during free time to climb at a place in the hills called The Shrine. I remember him asking me on the way up if I knew what a 'pitch' was. He explained how a big climb is broken into pitches so that a team of two can tackle it, swinging lead and follow. Little did I know it was a concept we would master and that would allow us to summit some of the most famous, thrilling, and enormous rock faces in America.

"As we fumbled around on the rocks that day, discovering how to move over stone, one thing stood out about Chris: his incredibly caring and supportive nature. He would spot me if I got stretched out traversing a section, encourage me when it got difficult, was never competitive, and would be the first to try a bold problem or route. This was a constant theme in my relationship with Chris over eleven years."

Soon after camp that summer, Chris and Greg discovered the South Platte River Basin. "The Platte changed our lives. It became our never-satiated climbing obsession. Back in those remote mountains, far from roads and other people, Chris would often say, 'I feel at home here.' He was so happy there, even after all his world-class climbing destinations. It was quality rock, scary routes, a lot of adventure, and just that sense of solitude, when you're the only one for miles and miles."

Greg observed that Chris had a simple approach to life. He didn't get frustrated, and he didn't focus on his limitations. He didn't wrestle unnecessarily with what he would do with his life. He just had faith that whatever came up for him would be right. As Greg said, "He was always, *This is my path; this is my joy.* Climbing was one of the greatest expressions of his constant pursuit of happiness and having fun.

"It's hard to encapsulate how Chris changed my life. It's pretty profound. I think Chris was completely engulfed in the moment. He seemed free of the kinds of questions and doubts that tend to occupy young people's minds— the 'should do's' and 'better do's' in life. Chris knew that life is about living, and he really savored his experience."

The stark beauty of red rock jutting out of a deserted landscape, on the drive home from Joshua Tree, up through Canyonlands National Park, matched the raw, empty feeling in my stomach. Chris's homeland was there, but he was not.

I never saw Chris climb. Actually, I did try a couple of times. Once, at the end of a canoe trip down the Colorado, I drove to the Black Canyon and met Chris and Greg at a climbers' camp. That night they spent the whole time getting ready—preparing a makeshift meal, spreading out climbing gear, searching through packs, totally absorbed. They said goodnight and left the next morning before I arose. As I hiked along a nature trail running beside the rim that day, I surveyed the looming black wall across the canyon. Somewhere on that precipitous, breathtaking expanse of rock were two forms moving. It was unsettling to realize what my son was doing. On the other occasion, Chris and I happened to be traveling in Canada at the same time, the August before he died. "I'd love to drive to Bugaboo Glacier Park on my way home to watch you climb," I said. But the timing was off. When I called Chris again, he was already home.

Chris is telling me to get outdoors more. To lighten up and have fun. Maybe I'll roam the West, show up at climbers' camps, and be camp cook. I'll tell stories and pass around a hat. I'll go out there without any goals or anticipation of return.

I once asked Chris how he knew what he knew at his age. He said, "I'm not really sure. I learned from you and Dad, of course. And I learned from others, especially Mr. Goody."

Mr. Goody, Chris's martial arts teacher, died just before Chris would have become a black belt in judo and karate. Two years later, after the official mourning period, as his family looked on, Chris untied his brown belt and received his black belt. He had been studying martial arts for almost ten years.

Through his college years, Chris continued to attend the same Saturday morning martial arts class for young people. There he sparred with black belts, helped teach the children, and served as an example. Chris applied the skill and discipline he acquired in martial arts to rock climbing. He learned the basics from one of the best climbers in the field.

Then the rock became his teacher, as he ascended on the strength of his fingers and learned to balance on an edge. In turn, Chris taught others to climb and was a model for intelligent climbing.

I like to think of Chris in Heaven welcoming children, encouraging them up slabs of light, some catching hold of his wings for a piggyback ride, teaching them to throw, flip, and fall through cloud.

Chris chose his teachers wisely. He learned to be self-reliant. He learned to trust. He learned to obey. He became his own teacher, guiding the child within. He learned to live by his own example, before he died.

Chris did not climb the day before he fell. In the evening he gathered with friends around the campfire. He listened, quiet and smiling.

As night descended over the camp, I received the golden light. Inside Chris, beneath all consciousness, his soul beamed love to me.

He had visited relatives across the country. He had gone by the martial arts school to see friends there. He had gathered his belongings from others and put everything in its place. In April he made his final car payment.

All the years of rock climbing had taught him the necessary confidence—how to push through uncertainty, how to be grounded while hanging in space, how to love in the deepest way, which gives spark to all that is.

The final hours were sacred hours. Chris was in his favorite place on Earth, among a circle of friends, smiling and comfortable. He thought of his mom, who had brought him into this life. He went to bed and woke up refreshed. The sun was peaking over the mountains, and it was a fine day for a climb.

Several of Chris's friends have told me about sudden feelings they have that he is with them. In September Chris's friend Steve was road cycling a loop near St. Vrain Valley in Hygiene, Colorado. A third of the way into the ride, a golden eagle swooped down and cruised with him, then flew to the top of a telephone pole. It flew on to the next and the next, perching up there each time Steve approached. As Steve turned and rode down into the valley, he looked to the side where the valley drops away, and the eagle was flying at eye level with him. It appeared six or seven times over the course of the sixty-mile ride.

Chris's friend Woody told me that on his birthday, he and his girlfriend were driving in the country. At sunset the sky turned neon colors, absolutely spectacular. He could feel Chris's presence. Suddenly an eagle came out of the sky. It was flying at eye level with him, slightly in front of the car, and then flew to the top of a telephone pole.

Others have experiences of Chris as a crow. Actually, Chris was nicknamed "The Crow" at work, as he was known for always knowing where to find free food. Chris's voice would come over the intercom, letting the bellmen know where the food was. "Caw-caw, caw-caw," the bellmen would respond. Since Chris has died, they tell me, crows often accompany them on hikes and bike rides, the places where they used to go with Chris. They caw at the crows, aware that Chris is with them.

My sister Diana, who moved to the Blue Ridge Mountains of North Carolina just before Chris's death, told me that her contractor, Donnie, was climbing a mountain on the day Chris died. He had walked to the edge of an outcropping when a crow flew up towards him, and he felt the presence of someone who had died. Several months later he was riding his bike when he saw two crows flying ahead of him and felt a surge of comfort concerning his marriage. Another day, as he was biking, a crow flew next to him for a long time. He was getting inspired messages like, *This is good! It's right here! Keep riding! Go, man!* Donnie is a little older than Chris, with similar appearance, lifestyle, and character. Somehow he knows the crows are Chris, even though he never met him.

A pair of crows lives in a tree 250 yards from Alan's house. They showed up after the eagles left last winter. Alan puts crackers on the railing, then whistles for them. Patricio, the smartest and most talented, picks up one cracker with his beak, takes it over to the second cracker, and places it on top. Then he picks up the two and carries them to the third, scoops the whole stack up in his beak, and flies to his nest.

Alan says you can see Patricio wind surfing. He and his mate chase off hawks. They fly above a hawk, then dive bomb and nip at its tail and wings. The other day Alan threw a chicken leg up on the hill, and in less than two seconds, Patricio came—vroom—and swooped it up. Alan said, "That was Chris."

Out of the shards of ruin come gifts unbidden. A breeze soothes my brow. Rain refreshes the garden. Everywhere I find smiling faces and safe passage through crowds. These are simple blessings. I am not alone.

Hand in hand with faith, I journey the river of my unknown. Currents take me; the channel shifts a thousand times, and yet the course is true. A kindred ray lights the way as I stream towards the wellspring from which I came, trusting in my deliverance.

Chris knew that deep reverent place of Partnership, beneath the vicissitudes of existence. He once said to a friend, "Have you ever noticed that when you reach the top of the mountain, no one is there to applaud you?" He followed the vibrant tenor of life and made it all the way home.

Only God knows how long we will be here. A short life is as good as a long one. All true paths lead home, and Chris was a fast walker.

"I am going to live the free life," Chris told friends on his last trip. He was an outdoorsman. He recognized his passion and pursued it. He knew he had what it takes. He lived simply, without fanfare. He revered nature. He was keenly observant.

Chris also meant that he was going to live life without a scheme. His life was going to be open-ended. He would go wherever life took him and partake fully in the offerings.

When Chris came to me on the second day after his death, he showed me that there are no divisions—not between life and death, being and doing, old and young. He showed me his truth. He showed me he was One.

Chris on top of spire, Cirque of the Unclimbables, Northwest Territories, Canada, August 2002.
Photograph © Jonny Copp / Coppworks.com, 2002.

I am going to live the free life. He meant he was going to live life without walls, in the fullness of light. He was at home in himself and at peace with the world.

February 25, 2004

Dear Greg,

I woke up this morning with a new understanding. Chris was changing. He was becoming more and more simplified. He was shedding tools and was down to a basic few. He was fast becoming the musician and the instrument. The last metamorphosis came when he died. He let go his body, leaving it to the rope swaying in the wind. Then he leaped, unleashing his soul to the harmony of the universe, at once a singular vibration and a piece of all creation.

Chris is the energy of nature. He may be a bird, a drop of dew, a flake of earth, or orange sky. He shifts with the wind and the tide. He can revert to pure essence whenever he wants. His enlightenment allows him this freedom.

Creative genius is the stuff of mythology—the omnipresent trickster just beyond our periphery—hidden within a rosebud or puff of cloud. To be sure, there is always some telltale sign. Chris's sign: the broad grin and chuckle at every turn.

Come May, I'm going to get in my car and head west to Yosemite. I'm going to take a comfortable tent, sleeping bag, cooking equipment, pad and pen.

Love,
Carol

8 YOSEMITE

I sense that Chris is becoming more involved in the cosmos. I wonder if he is moving further away. He has been close to us, but will it last?

The question is wrong. With the passage of time, though Chris may pursue the heights of Heaven, his light shines ever true. His voice becomes my voice, his breath mine.

I sometimes think that those who lose children are the lucky ones. We have been chosen by God to bear a cross. It can kill us or stir us. Out of the throes of heartbreak comes rebirth. I pull myself up, peek over the rim, and blink. Nothing is as I thought. I am humbled, and I am encouraged. Here I am, more willing to live on the edge, more willing to risk, to love and forgive. I follow wherever life takes me—to places I have never been before.

March 1, 2004

It feels daunting to go to Yosemite on the anniversary of Chris's death, to just take off in my car and go.

To look back on Chris taking off in his car last May and never coming home, and to repeat that action. It is an important step—but how can I prepare? Even to imagine that time last year is painful. How can I actually travel to the place where Chris lost his life? The memory puts me back in that time, imagining Chris in his Subaru.

I must keep in my heart the knowledge that Chris's soul knew he was going to die, that something spectacular happened, and it is cause for celebration. It is an anniversary celebration of a miracle. Going there will put me in touch with that miracle. It will be scary. I must go without expectation, stay with the truth of things as it unfolds, whatever it brings.

Last year there was a quickening in my awareness of Chris's impending death. That was then, and this is now. So it is not to relive that time but to see how things open up in this time.

Going to Yosemite isn't for the purpose of retracing Chris's path and invoking sadness. It is to stay with the beauty of the miracle, a deep respect, a tribute to Chris, and to stay with where he is today.

Once I knew I was going to Yosemite, it became the focal point of my life. I thought about it daily. I dreamed about it. It was the exciting unknown that lay ahead. Then, as winter began to lose its blustery grip, I learned that Teague Holmes was also going to Yosemite for the anniversary of Chris's death. We made our plans.

With the coming of spring, the shock of Chris's death had diminished, leaving me with a deeper realization of loss. I found myself wedged between two untenable worlds. Behind me, Chris's life on Earth was receding into the distance, while ahead lay a worrisome veil of uncertainty. I pined for his softness and playfulness, his sweet endearing personality, and feared the day when his spirit would also disappear, and all would be lost.

Bleak days were followed by blessed days, such divine sweetness, when the light of Heaven streamed through, and I would see with fresh eyes that Chris's death had been purposeful. It was always going to happen. He was always going home, so close to God he was, and I would just feel so happy for him, imagining his joy, while feeling his golden essence and the goodness and beauty of it all.

When all of life is glad again and bursting with exuberance, the tender buds of healing can peek through. Wondrously, in the midst of tumult came a steadying sense of closeness with Chris in my heart. I could be with friends without being overwhelmed with sadness. Most significantly, for the first time, I was taking a few of Chris's framed pictures out of the drawer where I had placed them and setting them out. Amid the pangs and birthing of spring, I created a shrine, which included pictures, a St. Christopher statue, Chris's climbing photo album, and an urn of his ashes.

There is something beautiful asleep inside of me. I'm given a lifetime to wake it up. To awaken the kernel of beauty, I must free the reins of resistance and surrender to the Way of things—as each moment comes to light and passes on. Otherwise, I will never get over Chris dying. I will miss the joy of wonder, never know the dawn.

There is something here for all of us, something to overcome. Chris didn't plan to die young, but he sensed he would. He would never see tigers in the wild. There were mountains he would never climb and races he would never win. He wouldn't grow old with people he loved. He could have clung to sorrow. Instead he chose to live.

Tomorrow lightning may strike. It matters not that the tree lives a thousand years and the moth a single day. What matters is waking up.

A year flies, hardly enough time to grieve the loss of a son.

Teague and I left Colorado heading west. Nestled among our goods are Chris's ashes, now in silk pouches for the hike to the summit of Half Dome, planned for May 31.

Teague, friend and climbing buddy, was with Chris then. Teague and I will be there together in Yosemite now in a spirit of celebration and remembrance.

We drove through California's Sierra Nevada, crossing over Tioga Pass to enter the uplands of Yosemite. Immediately upon entering the park, I could feel the sacredness of this ancient land of vast glaciated valleys and mountains shrouded in cloud—old, old spirits here. I blurted out, "Chris dwells here! This is Chris's home!" I imagined him among giants—ancient tribal peoples and the great naturalist, John Muir. I envisioned him being warmly welcomed into this sacred arena, reveling among enlightened souls.

From Tioga Pass the road leads through Tuolumne Meadows, a favorite climbing haunt of Chris's. The Tuolumne River meanders through a carpet of green felt. Dense forests reach up the mountains. Above the tree line, erratic boulders jut at every angle, stacking toward polished domes. I felt exhilarated and deeply moved.

As we headed down towards Yosemite Valley, some seventy miles away, Chris was with me, speaking soft words. *Relax, Mom. No need to be impatient or to worry. The timing of things will naturally unfold. You have done your part.*

May 26, 2004 – Camp 4, Yosemite

Living well is not so much about coming up with new themes. It is returning time and again to the same themes, more deeply. It is discovering new gems inside the truths I already know.

So I say again: all we have is now. All prior experiences are vanished. Like the writing on the inside bottom of my child's first cup, *All Gone.*

I say these things as I sit in Camp 4, realizing that life has moved on. There is a new crowd here. Very few met Chris, and none knew him well. Mostly these are people unaware of a dear death from among their ranks one year ago.

Teague took me under his wing, giving me the lowdown on how to get a spot in Camp 4. You slip in undetected the night before and get to the registration line early the next morning. The ranger office opens at 8:30. An hour after sunup I was there. I secured a campsite and was given a tag for the tent and a sheet of rules, one of which specified that all food and toiletries be stored in the bear boxes.

We pitched a yellow expedition tent, Chris's tent. "Yep, that's the one," said Teague. I had pulled it out of the mounds of mountain gear in Alan's garage the weekend before. It made for a cozy, spacious home. Teague preferred sleeping under the stars.

Camp 4 is Yosemite's legendary climber's camp. What makes it special is not physical beauty. It is basically a large dirt lot with shady trees, picnic tables, fire pits, two large bathrooms, communal sink, metal bear boxes, and bear-proof trash bins. It's the people who give this camp its character. Climbers worldwide come for the wonder of the geologic structures abounding in the valley. Many languages are spoken here. It is a real community. Climber or not, you feel a part of it. You feel included in this rich, reverent, humble family of able-bodied, peace-loving folks.

Bears mangle cars at the whiff of a lowly scent and carouse the camp while you sleep. One night a ranger came by announcing that a bear had ripped into the rear end of a Nissan. I heard the tent next to mine unzip, then, "Come with me, sir. You'll have to fill out a report." Later I awoke with a start, remembering the hand cream inside a shirt pocket. Through the night tramped the furry interlopers in dream upon dream.

Another night two rangers came with flashlights, looking for untagged tents. Footsteps and a beam of light slowly circled my makeshift home. It's a game. You are only allowed to stay in Camp 4 for a week. Climbers stay a month or longer, moving stealthily about. I imagined Chris playing the game effortlessly and with gusto.

May 27, 2004

If I dwell on Chris a year ago, the sensation of loss hovers. When I engage this moment, absence becomes presence—clouds dancing around the golden sun. Chris is with me.

May 28, 2004

How do I remember things worth remembering? Why celebrate an anniversary, when this moment is all that counts? Why be here in Yosemite at all, if Chris died a year ago?

Birth and death are miracles, each leaving an indelible mark on the soul. Birth is the flame sending us into the world, death the spark propelling us into the next.

The Universe knows when a soul, newly evolved from Earth, rejoins its Grace. On each anniversary the heavenly bodies align with that sacred moment, and there is rejoicing. Chris will be a yearling. Who knows what the recently reborn is up to. Uncork the champagne. May this and every anniversary be remembrance of hallowed flight through space.

May 29, 2004

We live long enough to learn the lessons our souls are here to learn. Along the way we share with others the wisdom we accrue. What an honor to die at age twenty-five! What an honor to die at any age. Believe me, I'm paying attention to my lessons. I trust the timing of my death will be just right.

We begin life close to spirit. Then we discover the world and run out to play. As we come closer to the end, spirit looms large again. This is the curve of a lifespan. We hurl into the heart of our lives, all the while moving seamlessly back to the roots.

Each night I cooked a meal for three or four amid stars, glowing campfires, laughter and chatter. Each night I crawled into my tent and stretched out listening to the music of clinking carabiners and many languages spoken in hushed tones. I included the cacophony of sound in my sphere of consciousness. It was soothing. I felt part of a grand world order. Each day I met more climbers, who welcomed me within their clan.

On Friday, Ammon McNeely showed up when Teague and I were cooking breakfast. "I'm so sorry you lost your son," he said. "It's a traumatic experience for us all when a brother goes." He said there would be a gathering of climbers in El Cap meadow later in the day. "Look for the big shady tree next to the path."

I made my way down the sandy footpath that Chris had walked just one year before. Sitting there among the brave and passionate, across from the sheer, awe-inspiring cliff of El Capitan, I began learning about climbing from the inside out.

Ammon introduced me to the others and told them that my son had died there the year before. None of them had known Chris, but most of them were aware of the climber who had been killed. They made me feel welcome among them.

I told them of my interest in climbing, as a way of better understanding my son. We sat in a circle, and I asked questions. Ammon and his friend Raphael LaGrange did most of the talking. Everyone listened intently. Everyone was compassionate.

Ammon had had a few close friends die in climbing accidents. It was hard, he said, when someone died climbing, but he knew that Chris wouldn't want me to quit living. He would want me to keep right on pursuing the things I love.

The climbers talked about how climbing is, on the one hand, a shared experience that creates a unique bond that is rare outside the climbing world. "One symbol of the partnership between climbers is the rope," Raphael told me. "It is the life connector, whether you are 60 feet apart or 200 feet apart. As the leader, you are putting your life into your partner's hands. Then you switch leads." On the other hand, as Ivo Ninov emphasized, climbing is a deeply personal experience. "Only that climber knows what it is," he said. "When you are climbing, you are by yourself. We shared this experience, but we cannot explain how we feel to anyone."

Climbing requires tremendous physical strength, but it is the mental aspect that makes the difference in climbing. "It's all about pushing what you think is possible for yourself," said Ammon. "Everyone who goes up there experiences fear and doubt. You have to push through those negative thoughts. You keep that focus and keep pushing. Sometimes there are legitimate reasons for those feelings. Reality is a fine line up there between being safe and being in a dicey, dangerous situation. The more you climb, the better you get at knowing when to back off and when to push through." He said that he applies what he learns in climbing to life. Climbing gives him the confidence to push through hard times and live life to the fullest.

"There are a community of sports," Raphael told me, "that share the same spirit, which includes climbing, surfing, and

FREEDOM TO FALL

sailing. Those are lifetime pursuits related to the natural environment. It's you versus something you can't control. Surfers can't control the wave. Climbers can't control the rock environment. What nature gives us, that's what we get. You have to know yourself to do really well. You have to know how you will react to pressure and variables you can't control. If you get hurt, you deal with it and learn."

There are two types of climbing, they told me, free climbing and aid climbing, and two corresponding mindsets. The aid climber uses gear that he has placed to ascend, while the free climber places gear only for protection and uses the rock to ascend.

"My specialty is aid climbing," Ammon said. "You put a piece of gear in a crack, clip your aider [runged webbing loops] to the gear, and climb up the aider. As you climb, you keep looking up to see where the route is headed. You put in another piece, clip your aider, and climb up again." He described how each crack is unique, and the climber has to determine what type and size of piece will fit in there, staying completely focused until he gets a placement that is solid enough to support his weight.

Ammon introduced me to his friend, Rob, who is a free climber. "Rob is a much better free climber than I am. He places gear, clips carabiners to the gear, and attaches a rope so in case he falls, it will arrest him. But he doesn't put his weight on the gear to climb."

When I said that I was reminded of the warrior spirit, which was Chris's philosophy, Ammon agreed that that is what climbing does. "It teaches you to be a warrior. There are so many emotions you go through on a hard climb—from fear and doubt, to excitement and elation, to suffering and pain. You keep pushing through all of that, and keep that focus. You forget about the things that constrict you and find strengths that you didn't know you had." Jared, a latecomer to the group, said that he experiences two kinds of freedoms in climbing, one being the journey when his concerns in life float away and all he is doing is climbing, and the other one being when he reaches the top and thinks about his life in a more meaningful way.

Raphael observed that while he abandons distractions to climb, he never abandons himself. "You find yourself," he said. "Before coming west three years ago, I told my family, 'Climbing gives me a lot in life. If anything ever happens to me, I want you to know that I was out doing the thing I love most.' Having told them that gives me peace of mind when I'm out climbing and going for it."

After Raphael said that, no one spoke for a long time.

It's not carelessness, I thought. *It's the opposite of that.*

May 30, 2004

The day approaches—the rebirth of my son into the spirit world. I do not know if I will feel something special or not. I do not even know if that day is important to him. I only know that being here now is good timing.

This morning so many people in the camp are greeting me. They know who I am and why I am here. They know tomorrow I will be hiking Half Dome to scatter Chris's ashes. I want to get an early start. I don't need to worry or hurry. I can take lots of rests on the way.

Lincoln Else was one of the two rangers first on the scene after Chris fell. We had spoken briefly on the phone in autumn. Later when I wrote him that I would be coming to Yosemite the last week of May, he wrote back that he would be returning to Yosemite that week, after a Mount Everest expedition, and was pleased that I would be there. On Sunday morning, the anniversary eve of the fall, we met in Camp 4, and Lincoln talked about the accident in detail.

"The Search and Rescue team in Yosemite is amorphous," Lincoln said. "When an accident occurs, the word goes out. Rangers, paid volunteers, and whoever else is available become the rescue team. This is a flexible group, not locked into an 'elite team' concept, but rather, 'Here is the challenge, who has the skills for what's needed?' There are 150 to 200 rescues per year. About twenty or thirty are technical climbing rescues, meaning where the terrain is difficult enough to require special climbing equipment. Ten to twelve fatalities occur per year in the park, for all types of reasons. The Park Service does it all—fire, rescues, arrests. There are no specialized teams confined to one department of service, although each ranger has his/her area of expertise."

Chris and his climbing partner that day, Sibylle Hechtel, began the Overhang Bypass route, on Lower Cathedral Rock, about nine in the morning.

Sibylle and Chris were halfway up the route, right next to Bridalveil Fall. Chris was leading. He had climbed above Sibylle and around a bend, out of sight. Suddenly Sibylle heard a call—*whoa*. It wasn't a yell, just a quick vocal reflex. The rope jerked tight, and she realized that Chris was falling. She caught the fall but couldn't see Chris. Bob, another climber, was free soloing the same route. He reached Sibylle five to ten minutes later, then climbed past Sibylle to a tree, where he could see Chris hanging 50 feet below in his harness, his rope caught around the tree.

Bob was able to speak to Chris. Chris told Bob he was having trouble seeing. Bob could see that Chris had fallen a long way. He knew he was hurt badly and needed help. He helped Sibylle calm down, then down climbed the route. Sibylle tied the rope to an anchor and climbed to the tree.

It was noon when Bob reached the Search and Rescue office. Keith and Lincoln, both climbing rangers, jumped into the car with climbing gear. They were the blitz team. A page went out on the radio. They reached Lower Cathedral. Through binoculars they could see Chris in his harness moving his arms. Lincoln and Keith began climbing the route. Other rangers and a big mix of people were gathering gear, medical equipment, and a litter to come up behind them.

At 1:30, Keith and Lincoln reached the tree. Five minutes before, their spotter, watching through binoculars, radioed that Chris had stopped moving and was slumped over backwards. They called to Chris. No response. Keith and Lincoln drilled anchor bolts in the rock. Keith, a medic, rappelled down to Chris and found him "unresponsive, pulseless, breathless."

The whole scenario shifted to a slower pace. Chris was lowered onto a litter, which was attached beneath a helicopter, and flown out. By this time a big crowd had formed at the base of the mountain.

Sibylle reported that Chris was well rested and in good spirits on the climb. The accident record mentions a stopper and carabiner clipped to the rope just above the harness, but what that meant wasn't clear. Either Chris placed an ineffective piece of protection that came out, or he hooked it to the rope after the fall. In a separate report for the American Alpine Club, "Accidents in North American Mountaineering, 2004," Lincoln wrote, "Details suggest that he clipped this piece to the rope after his fall in order to secure his backpack."

The cause of the accident is unknown. We only know that Chris was climbing with little protection on moderately difficult, craggy terrain—well within his comfort range. It is hard to find suitable spots for gear placement on that route, and he may have been saving his gear. His goal was Overhang Overpass, a more challenging route ahead. "It's a constant debate in the mind of the climber, whether to place gear or not. You only have so much," Lincoln said. "Chris may have felt he didn't need it."

We will never know whether Chris made a mistake, or a rock gave way, or some play of fate happened that cannot be imagined. There were no witnesses. It simply will never be known. The cause of death is also unknown. No autopsy was performed, in accordance with our wishes. Most likely he died from head injury. The rock in that area slopes away in a series of slabs and ledges, so Chris would have hit ledges on the way down. His left temporal region was severely swollen, and there was trauma to his chest. Though Chris was not wearing a helmet, a helmet probably would not have saved him. Helmets, a matter of personal choice, were at that time designed to protect mainly from rockfall rather than from frontal or side injury.*

I do not know whether or not he experienced pain. If he did, it is okay. Physical pain is forgotten as soon as it is over. I did not take an anesthetic when I gave birth. I never thought of that pain afterward; the pride and joy that followed is all I know. The joy and freedom following death is what Chris knows.

Lincoln took me to Lower Cathedral. He located the area by this slice of sun, that tree, this ledge, that slope, this glint, that dark crevice. He indicated the line of fall, over the tree. I saw where Chris came to rest. The spot he fell from is not known, will never be known. I felt closure—a viewing of concrete reality that brought acceptance.

May 31 rose like a breeze in the tropics. Teague and I left camp and headed for Half Dome, the gigantic stone monolith that Chris and Teague had climbed days before Chris died.

Soon we became soaked by the spray of waterfalls tumbling down the mountain. Up and up we climbed, circling the 4,000-foot giant on an 8½-mile journey by trail towards the summit. I scaled steep stone steps and trod through forests of tall, sturdy pines and cedars, sandy flats, lush meadows, streams and pools, sweating, straining, putting one foot in front of the other.

Chris, are you sure? I may be too old.

* John Long states in *How to Rock Climb!* (2004), in reference to wearing a helmet, "Acts of God notwithstanding, safety largely lies with the climber, not in his or her gear."

Mom, I'm sure. Lean into your steps. Shed clothing behind a rock. The weather is fine today.

High above, wisps of cirrus clouds formed. We went around a bend and emerged from forest into the wide open. Alongside the trail the rock sloped gently down before plunging to the valley floor. We were on the rim, the glorious rim!

Across the canyon was a series of mountains, perfect likenesses of one another, indigo and snowcapped. I stood and looked: The peaks were delicate, whimsical, at once striking and droll, as if the wind had playfully tossed ice cream cones on the mountaintops.

As I started to turn back to the trail, my eye was caught by bands of rainbow colors stretched across the sky. I glanced at my watch—high noon.

"Teague, look! What is that?!"

"I don't know. There's no moisture. I've never seen anything like it."

It began to dawn on me. "It's Chris—*it's Chris!*"

In the weeks before the journey to Yosemite, I had felt a gathering of forces. I sensed there might be a sign on Half Dome on the day of Chris's death. But by the time we arrived, I had forgotten about that. I was thinking about the scattering of ashes. As the anniversary day approached, I rested, ate judiciously, and eyed Half Dome, brilliantly lit in the late afternoon sun.

Hiking up that stone titan, I had been putting one foot in front of the other; that was all. So when we stepped around that bend onto the rim and the colors appeared, it took a moment to know what I was seeing. At noon, a veil lifted between this world and the next.

Half Dome, Yosemite National Park.
Photograph © Doug Thomson, 2009.

Teague sat down in the bright sunlight. I walked towards the edge of the canyon, to the shade of a lone tree.

The sky moved in close around me, filling with a kaleidoscope of neon-lit clouds. I was sitting center stage surrounded by gigantic turquoise waves splashing high, orange ripples, red swirls, patches of peach, indigo, green, yellow, blue, and violet piled fluffily on top of one another. A textured wall climbed up the middle in iridescent bands of brilliant color. Great sheets of white cloud spilled through the shifting diorama, forming resplendent valleys and slopes. I would be looking at one scene, then realize I was seeing another, so seamlessly they moved. The sky was dancing! It was my son, winging the void: beautiful, blissful, silent, sacred.

Gradually the colors faded, streaks lingering at the base of a cloud. A half hour had passed by. I walked towards Teague and peered at the sun. It was glowing in the pure blue, arced by rainbow colors.

After that, there really was no need to continue up. Chris had met me on the trail. But it was in my mind to spread the ashes from the summit.

Such a struggle! The trail became a series of steep, stone switchbacks. People were moaning, collapsing on the steps. I stopped and leaned against a wall, unable to move, seeking comfort for my throbbing legs. Determination returned and I struggled on behind Teague. Finally my foot landed on the sturdy, broad outcropping of Half Dome's shoulder.

Ahead lay the last hunk of sheer rock leading to the summit, the half dome of Half Dome. There were cables to aid hikers in the intimidating ascent. *Chris never intended this,*

I thought, feeling reluctant to go. We rested, and from my bag I retrieved a caffeinated power gel. An ounce of energy boosted my spirits and courage. "I'm going for it," I said.

I started up the cables. Teague followed, prepared to catch me if necessary. Halfway there the rock turned vertical! My hands began slipping, and I clutched the cables. Whimpering, I told Teague I couldn't go any farther. We backed all the way down to the shoulder. I gave a pouch of ashes to Teague. He scrambled up the rock outside the cables, passing brave stuck souls. He was on the summit for half an hour.

Meanwhile, I watched ravens diving, soaring, and flipping like black angels, elemental, sleek, pure. At that altitude among granite gods, the raucous call was entirely appropriate, a crying out of blessed felicity. Above the ravens floated a ribbon of rainbow color.

Teague had a beautiful experience, he told me when he came down. He was honored and touched by the scattering of ashes, which he sent cascading down the same route he and Chris had climbed together one year ago.

Two pouches remained. We returned to the place of the miracle. I ran out on the rock and began scattering the ashes, hurrying from place to place until they were gone. I opened my arms wide to the heavens. My journey was complete. A deep satisfying peace glowed within.

The 8½-mile trek down seemed to take twice as long. My whole body ached. The weather held, clouds and breeze taking the edge off a high sierra summer afternoon. We drenched ourselves at the waterfalls and arrived at the car at dusk. Fourteen hours had elapsed in the journey. We went for pizza, the best I ever ate, then drove back to camp. I climbed inside my sleeping bag and stretched out. No thoughts, just drifting, drifting into tranquil sleep.

Early the next morning I woke up refreshed. I wasn't even sore! Rob, the free climber I had met in El Cap Meadow, came over to my camp to ask about the hike.

"I didn't make it up that last little bit," I told him. "But Chris met me on the path. He filled the sky with rainbow colors."

Rob shot me a look of recognition. "I saw the colors," he said. "I was on top of another mountain. A storm was moving in, and then it didn't happen. It was strange. There were bands of rainbows scattered across the sky."

9 AT OVERHANG BYPASS

In the fall of 2003, I had talked briefly by phone to Sibylle, Chris's climbing partner on the day he died. She had said then that she hoped to be able to speak with me and with Alan, but a year passed before we sat down together at her home in Silver Plume, in the mountains close to Breckenridge. She was warm, welcoming, and open.

Sibylle was the only witness to Chris's death. Undoubtedly, she was traumatized by the experience. It took her a long time to climb again. But I also sensed in her a steadfastness and inner strength.

Sibylle had gone to Yosemite that May for the grand opening of "Vertical Frontier," a movie about the history of Yosemite climbing. She had a small part in the movie because she and a friend were the first women to climb El Capitan. After the movie, as they were filing out, she met Chris, and then one evening in Camp 4, he asked her to climb.

The next day they climbed the Kor-Beck, a long route near the east buttress of Middle Cathedral. Chris led the hard pitches and spotted Sibylle down climbing a steep gully, where a fall would have meant going to the bottom. A rockfall the year before had sheared off bolts used for rappelling, and the gully was littered with huge boulders. "I was thrilled that he was willing to down climb first and spot me—a big, tall, strong, young guy." At fifty, Sibylle was twice his age.

After that first experience together, Sibylle felt comfortable climbing other routes with Chris.

"He was so helpful, courteous, and cheerful. I really liked climbing with him. We were already pals. Once we found out we lived in nearby towns, we made plans to go all over the place climbing. Chris wasn't so serious. Unlike a lot of climbers at his level, he was interested in climbing anything and everything, not just difficult routes.

"He had seen the movie 'Vertical Frontier' and was so excited about meeting some of us who were in the movie, because we were considered 'historical figures.' Chris was fascinated by the history of Yosemite climbing. That was the main reason he asked me to climb with him."

One day Chris approached Sibylle about climbing two contiguous corner routes on Lower Cathedral Rock. The first route, Overhang Bypass, went up to a roof, swung left, then back up the mountain, while the second, more difficult route, Overhang Overpass, continued up the corner. That was the route Chris was interested in. But Sibylle had an injured finger and didn't want to commit to it, because it would mean having to take out gear that he placed on a route involving

Chris relaxing with friends in Camp 4, Yosemite National Park, May 2003.
Photograph © Chris Hampson, 2009.

finger-crack climbing. So Chris suggested that they traverse around on Overhang Bypass, get to the top of Overhang Overpass, and from there they could top-rope it. They could set an anchor at the top and take turns rappelling down and climbing up without the need to place and remove gear.

They left camp at eight in the morning. "We didn't take a lot of gear because it was an easy route, and we were going to top-rope the hard part. The trail leading to the climb was steep and filled with rubble. I was grabbing rocks and branches to pull myself up, gasping and wheezing, while Chris was way up there, racing along full hilt. When we finally reunited I said, 'Chris, I don't stand a chance of keeping up with you.' He laughed, saying, 'You know, just the other day, Teague was telling me that he was having trouble keeping up with me going *downhill*.' So of course when I got to the base of the climb, Chris had his climbing shoes on and was all ready to go. He led the first pitch, winding around a corner to a gulley, and belayed me up."

The morning air was brisk, and they both wore windbreakers. On the second pitch, Sibylle, who was leading, came to the roof, traversed left under the roof, and climbed up a ways to a little sloping ledge. She sat down and began putting in gear for an anchor. Chris was about 15 feet below her. She called down, "Hey, Chris, why don't you give me your gear?" She wanted to put in a third piece to strengthen the anchor. Chris handed up the gear and stayed put for a little while to enjoy the view. They were right above Bridalveil Fall, and it was sending out a big spray with a rainbow. Sibylle secured the anchor with another piece, tied the pieces together with runners, and ran the rope through the anchor to her belay device. Then she leaned over and said, "Hey, Chris, now we have a really bomber anchor. You never know when someone is going to take a big ripper [fall]." Chris called up, "Yeah, but we know that isn't going to happen today, don't we?"

There was a pause in Sibylle's story. We looked at each other. "Yeah, I know," she said. "I still get chills."

Chris climbed up to the shelf where Sibylle was. It would be his lead. He looked ahead. To the left was a ramp—low angled and easy to clasp—that diagonaled up a long way to a ledge that went straight across above them. Chris said, "I'll just head left up the ramp until I hit the ledge and go back right to that tree over there. I probably won't put in very much gear." "The route zigzagged back and forth," Sibylle explained. "You don't want to put in very much gear if you're going this way and that way, because you are going to get rope drag. It was all easy, anyway."

Chris headed up and around the corner. Here and there he would put a runner around a tree, clip a carabiner to it, and clip the rope to the carabiner. Then she couldn't see him anymore. "I'm feeding out the rope. He runs it out and he runs it out, and he goes and he goes. Suddenly I heard a whoop, and soon afterwards there was a tug on the rope." It was around ten, Sibylle thought. They had been climbing for about an hour.

Sibylle didn't know why he fell. She guessed that a piece of rock, one that he was standing on or possibly reaching for, came out of the mountain. Lower Cathedral is known, she said, for rocks that come loose. "I was sitting there in total shock because I knew he had fallen a long ways. I only had 20 feet left of my 180-foot rope, so basically he fell 150 feet—and he wasn't moving. Usually, after someone falls, they try to get on their hands and feet to get the weight off the end of the rope and get up on a ledge or a foothold. That wasn't happening."

Within five minutes Sibylle's friend Bob Jensen showed up, free soloing the route. The year before Sibylle had worked for Yosemite Search and Rescue, and Bob had worked for Tuolumne Search and Rescue. He was an emergency first responder.

Sibylle sighed with relief. "Oh, Bob, thank God you are here. My partner just took a fall, and he isn't moving."

Bob asked for his name, then climbed up along the rope 70 or 80 feet to a tree. The rope was looped around the tree, and Chris was hanging in his harness 50 feet below it.

Bob yelled down, "Chris, can you hear me?"

"Yeah, I can hear you," Chris said, in a clear voice.

"There is a ledge 15 or 20 feet above you. You'll be a lot more comfortable if you can get to the ledge. Can you try to climb up to the ledge?"

Chris answered, "Yeah, I can try, but I can't see very well."

"Do you think you broke something? Where do you hurt?" Bob asked him.

"I kind of hurt all over," Chris said.

Bob, visibly shaken, down climbed to Sibylle and told her that he thought Chris had a life-threatening head injury, and he was going to go get Search and Rescue. He told Sibylle to climb to the tree and see what she could do.

Sibylle took the rope out of the belay device by attaching prusiks [movable slings] to the rope, then tying the prusiks into the anchor. Now the rope was going straight to the anchor. "It took me 30 to 45 minutes to get that system set up safely. Most people without search and rescue training can't do it. All of Chris's weight was hanging on the other end of the rope. I had to very carefully transfer all that weight back and forth, from the belay device to the prusiks and from the prusiks into the anchor. You can't make a single mistake. Then I put two more prusiks on the rope to help me climb to the tree, so that I was safe.

"When I got to the tree, I called down, 'Chris, Chris, can you try to climb up?' I attached the prusiks to the section of rope leading down to Chris, to see if I could pull him to the ledge. The thing is, he's 200 pounds."

Some climbers were coming up the route. Sibylle alerted them that her partner was injured, and there wasn't room to pass. While they tied themselves in below, she borrowed their rope—cautiously down climbing to grab the end of it and dragging it up—with the idea of rappelling down to Chris. But there were no suitable rock features to anchor it to, only the one tree, mostly dead and covered with mistletoe. It wasn't a risk worth taking. With mounting distress, she realized that even if she were able to reach him, probably she couldn't have moved him

"I kept thinking, *What am I going to do?* I was pacing back and forth on a shelf, saying, 'Come on, Chris, come on. Let's see if you can get up. Try to climb while I pull.' And I would pull while he moved his arms trying to lift himself so he could climb to the ledge. He was off route, hanging on a sort of blank slope. It didn't look easy. If he could have gotten his weight off the rope, I could have pulled on the slack to give him tension higher up."

About eleven o'clock the sun hit them, and it was getting hot. Chris took off his backpack and clipped it in front of him. Sibylle thought he was trying to get water, but either he couldn't see or couldn't manipulate the zippers. "There he was in the blazing sun with a dark windbreaker, trying to get water. Time was passing, and I was desperate to get him out of the harness and onto the ledge. I felt really bad. I felt like there should have been something I could have done. . . .

"Chris was in character the whole time. I couldn't believe it. So many times I've seen a climber take a minor fall and get angry. Chris didn't do that. We talked here and there. Towards the end he was waving his arms and saying, 'When is this going to stop? When is this going to be over?' But he was just saying those things. There was no outburst. He must have really been in pain then. I was totally upset hearing this, and I called down, 'Hang in there, Chris; hang in there.'"

Five minutes later—three or more hours after the fall—Search and Rescue arrived. They drilled bolts in the rock, and Keith climbed down.

"The thing I've always wondered about," Sibylle said, "was, did he know? Did he know the extent of his injuries?" I told her that I didn't believe he was calculating those things. "Good," she said. "But I really did not expect him to die. I really didn't, because when Bob called down to him and he answered, he sounded cheerful. He was the same as he always was. Chris was always civil, patient, and good-natured, and he maintained that to the end."

What I am left with, beyond the tears that the story of Chris's death always brings, is Sibylle's bravery and moral support to Chris that day. While she encouraged Chris not to give up, she herself never gave up. She was the voice of comfort and hope, giving to Chris what he had always given to others.

After Sibylle returned home to Colorado, she wrote to friends who had climbed with Chris in Yosemite, seeking information for an obituary she was writing for "Rock and Ice Magazine." She received many kind responses. Susan Sheffield, whom Chris had been planning to meet at another climbing location the weekend after his fall, wrote back:

"I knew Chris only a short time, yet he showed me so much beauty. Confident, handsome, generous, Chris thought of those around him as much as he did himself. My friend Holly and I spent a day climbing with him at Collie Cliff, a beautiful sunny day. We chatted, shared lunch, and I watched him float up Catchy Corner. His infectious smile and gentle, calm nature inspired me.

"How Chris died seems so random to me. Running it out on easy terrain, a route that he could have easily free soloed—that could happen to any of us. We'll never know what really happened or why. I watched his rescue from El Cap Meadow, without imagining it could ever be him. Chris was always giving without expecting anything in return, and knowing him for a short time was a gift."

When Chris's spirit left Overhang Bypass that day, apparently he had a little more climbing to do. Matt Miller told me that he was climbing in the Grand Teton of Wyoming that afternoon, just starting up the last pitch. An operation on an injured shoulder the winter before was causing him to feel tentative, and he wondered if he could do it.

Matt looked back at Mount Owen and thought, *When Chris swings back this way, I'm going to bring him up here.* They had climbed Lunar Ecstasy in Zion National Park together a few weeks earlier. "Chris put a lot of faith in me on that climb, my first since the operation. He was so brave, patient, and encouraging. We had a great time. Chris left for the rest of his trip, and I went on to the Grand Teton. He was planning to meet me there on his way home from Yosemite."

As Matt ascended the route, he was protecting his shoulder, and it held him back. Suddenly he felt Chris's presence, right behind him, tapping him on the shoulder. He decided he was just going to climb. With each move, he could feel Chris tapping. He let go of the shoulder. A great freedom opened up, and he reached the top of the mountain.

When Matt came down from the climb, there was a message on his cell phone from a friend. He called back, and the friend said, "I have some bad news. Chris died today in a rock climbing accident." *But he was there!* Matt thought. *He was right there with me!*

Chris had promised Matt. It was one last climb, on his way home to God.

10 BEYOND THE HIGH SIERRA

When it has been too long since I've heard his voice or seen the sparkle in his eye, what can I do? Bring myself back, and stay the course.

For many seasons I have floated in the pure liquid mirror of God's grace in the afterglow of my child's death. Though my bond with Chris is constant and stronger than gold, I cannot linger much longer. His vibration becomes higher and finer, and somewhere outside this sanctuary, faintly calling, is the semblance of a life I used to love.

Where do I step after my loss? With each passing day, the earth draws me back. The air feels refreshing, as after a rain. After the absence, I see more clearly Earth's surface and the myriad shapes around me. I see that my path is uniquely my own, crossing many other paths. I see that we are one splendor and the splendor of infinite forms.

The clouds that were bordering the refuge disperse, and I find myself on the brink of the space beyond, trusting the road ahead.

Two weeks before Christmas, I drove out to the countryside and bought a King Charles spaniel, commonly called the English toy. It's a rare breed. I named her Megan. Overnight she became my best friend.

Megan won the heart of everyone who met her. She was the cutest dog I'd ever seen—huge black eyes, long floppy ears, pug nose, with patches of black and white and splashes of copper. She looked and acted like a clown. When Kate came home for the holidays, she fell in love with her. "Mom," she said, "Little Megan is perfect for you. She even looks like you."

Alan came over to visit Kate. I was away getting groceries, and when I returned, Megan was in Alan's lap. "I like your dog," he said. He noted how calm she was and how she didn't bark. It was the first time I saw Alan take an active interest in something since Chris died.

I seemed to be having an allergic reaction to Megan, but I wasn't sure. I called Alan and asked if he might be interested in buying her from me. I offered to hand her over to him for a week, with the understanding that I could take her back. Alan said he would take her. The next day I called to say that I had changed my mind. I was feeling better, I told him, and besides, I loved her too much. "But you said!" he exclaimed. "No, Alan, I said we would try it out. I didn't promise. I'm sorry. There is another adorable puppy in the litter." "No!" he said emphatically. "It's this dog or no dog. I would be willing to buy your dog, but I won't go out and get another one."

One morning before dawn, as Megan and I played in the backyard, the pale beauty of a star to the south caught my eye. I tossed Megan out into the snow and looked up again. There was a steady white light slightly overlapping the star that I hadn't seen before. That day an idea emerged. On Christmas day I handed Megan to Kate, and said, "Take the puppy to your dad. Tell him I said, 'Merry Christmas.'"

Two days later I drove up to Alan's house to visit Megan. I still felt bonded to her and wondered if I had made the right decision. She was overjoyed to see me. We played fetch. She streaked around the house barking excitedly, leaped high, and passed back and forth between my legs. She sat in my lap. I'd look down and she'd look up, ears out, eyes gazing into mine. Alan looked at me, his eyes questioning. "We were quite the pair," I sighed.

Megan has become Alan's constant companion. They take long walks together. She accompanies him to the office. She is a pocket-size bundle of love, giving to Alan what neither I nor any human could give him.

We have lived through two Christmases without Chris, but still he sends gifts. This year's gift was for his dad, the best Christmas present I ever gave.

January 17th was Chris's birthday. I recognize the angle and quality of sunlight through the crisp, bare, windblown air.

I went on a hike to celebrate Chris in nature. Following a climbers' trail in Boulder's Chautauqua Park, I came to a place where climbers were just starting up and sat on a slab of sun-baked rock, enjoying the unusually fair day. On the way back down, the rap of a woodpecker caught my attention. Woodchips were flying. *There's Chris,* I thought. On the way home I cried.

Kate called in the afternoon to see how I was doing. I told her about giving birth to Chris—the labor that started in the night and how I thought it was indigestion because the next day was my due date, and I didn't believe a child would be so punctual. I told her about the pushing and breaking of blood vessels in my face and then—it's a boy!

She told me that she had no memory of anything special Chris ever said or did to show his love to her. What she remembered was his being mean or ignoring her. I explained that that is typical of first-born children, especially when they are two years older. But often, I told her, siblings become closer later in life.

Kate could see that happening among her friends; they were beginning to be good friends with their brothers and sisters. And that left her sad: Chris had started opening up to her during his last year, calling her and including her in his life. And then he died.

I reminded Kate of something I'd said before, that even though her brother wasn't always nice to her, he loved her and was now helping to guide her from a higher plane.

"It's true, Mom," she said. "The day Chris died, my life began to improve. The family was in crisis, and I had to pull myself together. My life has been improving ever since. I am amazed by all the good things that have happened and how my life has fallen into place."

"You have your whole life in front of you," I said. "These are wonderful years. Chris will always be there for you, but you are going into the heart of your life. As you grow older, you will feel a deepening connection with Chris."

"Just before Chris died," she said, "when I was having a crisis and you came out to California to be with me, I had the thought one day that you are a petite woman, yet you are a pillar of strength. Then Chris died, and I saw you so shaken. And now, seeing you at Christmas, and giving little Megan to Dad, you are a pillar of strength again. I love you so much, Mom."

"I love you too, Kate."

When a child comes forth into the world, an imprint is made of two tiny feet, an heirloom token of a momentous event. At the same time an imprint is made on the soul of mother and child, a tacit token of an unbreakable bond. Through the nurturing that follows, the child grows.

When the second child comes along, the exclusivity between the first-born and the mother is disrupted. I talked with my toddler about the child growing inside my belly. Then one night as the time drew near, Chris stood up, and through a ramble of half formed words and gesturing, enacted the birth scene of baby coming down the tunnel and out into the world. But I couldn't prepare him for that disruption.

A few weeks after Kate was born, Chris left with his dad to visit his grandma in New Mexico. I was nursing Kate on the couch in the living room when they returned. The front door opened, and a tiny ball of black fur darted in, followed by Chris. He didn't look at me; with outstretched arms he was running after his new kitten. At age ten, he wrote in his "Life Story" that when he was two, a "tragedy" happened, the birth of his sister.

Shortly after Christmas of 2001, just before Kate left to return to school in San Francisco, she said, "Mom, Chris didn't pay attention to me when I went up to Breckenridge. Christie and I stayed at his house, but he didn't stick around. He didn't take me places or introduce me to his friends. He didn't ski with me. I feel hurt because I went up there to be with him."

I called Chris and told him that Kate was upset. "But she came up here to ski with Christie!" he protested. "Yes, she went up to ski," I said, "but the real reason she went was to spend time with you. She loves you, Christopher, and you excluded her and hurt her feelings." There was silence, and then, "Okay, Mom."

After that day, Chris changed towards Kate. The next Christmas when Kate went skiing in Breckenridge, Chris showed her around and introduced her to his friends. Kate was thrilled. Chris became the brother Kate always wanted—but only got to experience for a little while.

There were times in growing up when Chris took pleasure in Kate's company, times he put his arm around her or threw her up on his shoulders. He was proud of her piano playing and went to all of her recitals. When she started art school and began applying herself in earnest, he was pleased. He would brag to friends about her talent and relished the art she gave him. One piece she gave him as a Christmas gift needed a little finish work. He was after her about it until she finished it, and then he hung it over the mantel in the most prominent place in his house.

Belatedly Chris admitted his unfairness to Kate. It was a blind spot. It was the last thing he needed to learn, and the last bit of parenting I ever did.

All children outgrow the imprint of two tiny feet. And children, under the best of circumstances, let disillusions go. Mothers let their children go. Birthdays come and go. But the imprint on the soul remains constant, for the mother and each precious child.

May 15, 2005

As the second anniversary of Chris's death approaches, I become restless. The May light, tinged with sorrow, pervades my awareness, as one day slips quietly into another. Suddenly, remembrance comes bustling in like a familiar friend. Out of nowhere on the eve of Chris's death came the golden light.

On my dresser is a framed picture of Chris sitting in a grassy field. It is a picture he took of himself days before he died. He radiates serenity and well-being. When I see him thus, so centered and at peace, all doubt fades away.

Each time I affirm what I know, a stone is laid. After two years, I have attained a solid foothold.

May 31 is our day to celebrate. Just imagine where Chris is now! Of course it is beyond imagining, but the glistening presence I feel as we come closer is an indication. All is well and as it should be.

May 20, 2005

In matters of God, proof has no place. *It does not matter,* I hear Chris say.

It doesn't matter if I knew or not. No knowledge of future events can stand up to living in the present. I stood in the center of possibility—embracing this moment, reaching for the next, not knowing where it would take me. If I had knowledge, it became irrelevant. I was thankful for each day, and when I was dying I was thankful for all that I had been given.

There is no compromise when you live on this pinpoint in time. You don't need slogans. When you are fully alive, each day is the last. You only need one. Each day is as much composed of Essence as the next.

It was never for me to say when I might die. I am thankful for the life I was given. I am thankful for the freedom I have now. This is home, where I am close to God.

May 30, 2005

Yesterday and today the sky has been overcast, with rain yesterday afternoon. This morning is quite cool. The earth smells sweet and fresh. Chris's energy is very present. It is a subtle, refined energy, all gold. It requires stillness to tap into it. There is a feeling of sacredness pervading the crisp spring air.

Once, Chris gave his dad two river rocks for a birthday present. As he unloaded the rocks from his car, he said, "These met my two criteria: cheap and close at hand."

Chasing after purpose is like chasing a phantom. It comes and goes and gets lost in the shuffle. It's an illusion. It holds out promise—the carrot just out of reach.

You have to be able to say, "This isn't working," and shift. Ask yourself, "How do I feel? How connected am I to what is happening right now?" Be willing to turn things around, try life a different way. It's the only chance you have to bump into reality. That is the path. When you find it, have the wherewithal to recognize it and stay on it. It is the path that is meant for you.

Sometimes I think God put the loss of Chris in my path to shake me up. Perhaps I needed this jarring experience to bring me back to earth. It is my genuine task not to hold Chris's death in front of me as one more thing—keeping me from my life.

The best reality is the experience of opening up to what I already have. Sooner or later, honest work starts to kick in. I have climbed. I haven't tried to get somewhere by magic. I haven't taken easy street.

No one else will ever know. My steps leave no trace. It is my sweat, my blood, my tears, my gifts, my joy. The texture of real experience is irreplaceable. This is my trail and the jewels I reap along the way: cheap and close at hand.

On May 31, I went with Greg and Sarah to the South Platte, a richly forested river basin with spectacular outcroppings of jumbled rock formations, accessed by a labyrinth of dirt roads. It was in this hinterland of rugged beauty that Chris had nurtured his passion.

To get back to the area where we wanted to be, we had to cross a swollen, roaring creek. Greg located a spot where a log lay across the creek to a rock, from which you could jump to land. A foot above the log was an old faded climbing rope, stretching loosely from a big root bulging out of the steep embankment on our side to a tree on the far side.

"This is Chris's old rope, his first climbing rope! It's the exact same rope as the one he used when we first discovered the South Platte!" Greg exclaimed.

"St. Christopher must be here to help us across," I remarked.

Greg braved the river crossing, stepping sure-footedly along the log. Then jaunting back and forth, he anchored his rope to tree limbs on either side and pulled it taut above Chris's rope. Sarah and I stepped into climbing harnesses, which Greg clipped to his rope. Then sliding our hands along his rope, using Chris's rope as foot leverage, we crossed the raging river. I named this place "Chris's Crossing."

While Sarah and Greg climbed, I napped by the river and hiked. It was a gorgeous day with a hint of coolness and sporadic cloud cover, the first fair day after a week of rain. Just before dusk, we watched the sun emerge gloriously among clusters of pastel cloud mosaics.

Meanwhile, Kate went to West Ranch, the mountain community where she grew up, carrying her urn of Chris's ashes. Kate made our urns in the weeks following Chris's death. Each urn is uniquely shaped and glazed. We lined them up and chose the ones we wanted. Kate's is a portrait of sky—shades of aquamarine and fleecy white clouds.

Her plan was to scatter the ashes on Ladybug Hill, the old haunt she most associates with Chris, christened by our family for the ladybugs shrouding the big granite boulders overlooking the valley. The forest trail leading to Ladybug Hill was gone, and a couple of houses had sprung up in the area. She persevered, asking for guidance with each step, and at last the big red rocks loomed ahead. She spread Chris's ashes on the rocks and filled her urn with wildflowers.

Kate brought the flowers home and put them on the kitchen table along with some keepsake stones. She said, "Mom, smell the flowers. They smell just like West Ranch," and they did.

Each day Kate was here in Colorado with us, she talked more freely about Chris, and I watched her come more to terms with his death. Chris has been with Kate in a special way this trip: She's a college graduate.

Kate said Ladybug Hill was just as she remembered it. She had a wonderful experience. You could see her glow.

After that anniversary, I was sad. It was a renewed feeling of loss. I was realizing that there is not this one long line where you move perpetually towards recovery; at least that isn't my experience. I visit grieving time and again. Each time it is different. I see the maturity on the faces of Chris's friends. Soon they will be marrying, having families, and growing older. It is such a vital wound, the loss of a child. My spiritual connection with Chris has sustained me. I have seen deeper and deeper into reality, as it comes through my experience of Chris's death. Yet here I am, crying all over again. There is no substitute for grieving. No matter how far I've come, there is more.

There is no one who brings joy the way your own child does. You revel in the aliveness of your own child and the miracle of his being. You take pleasure in his pleasure and feel hurt when he is hurt. To lose a child is one of the most profound experiences of human life.

I go to the mirror and have a talk with Chris. It is much like the talks I had with him two years ago, yet not with the same raw pain as then. I say, *Christopher, maybe you should have considered the impact your death would have on others. Maybe this is something you need to learn, and you are learning it now by witnessing. I want to hold you, laugh with you, and hear your deep affectionate voice. Do you see, Christopher?*

My words are not words of anger. I have never been angry at Chris for dying. They are words of regret. The regret will dissipate with the morning sun; it always does. The goodness of our love will be with me again, my faith restored. But I can't unfalteringly keep to higher ground. Loss is real. This too is my truth, at this moment in time.

11 "WE TAKE THESE RISKS"

On a spring evening, shortly after the second anniversary of Chris's fall, Greg accepted an invitation to my house for dinner and an interview. Though our friendship endures, it would be the last time I solicited his help in understanding Chris as a climber.

From the beginning Chris was a free climber, Greg told me. He said there are two ways to climb rocks free: traditional and sport. In sport climbing, the routes—typically within easy reach—are pre-bolted and have solid anchors on top. The climber clips the bolts as he goes along, and the furthest he can fall is five or ten feet. It allows one to practice challenging moves in short periods of time, so that progress is achieved with minimal risk and without the factor of the unknown. Traditional climbing, on the other hand, is the reverse. It's all about climbing into the unknown where the risk factor may be great, often in faraway settings, difficult to access. The climber places his own pieces of protection, while regarding the course of the route; then his partner takes the pieces out as he follows up. There are no safety nets or guarantees. Chris, Greg said, was a traditionalist at heart.

Traditional climbing, I learned, is based on the mentality of the "golden era." In the 1950s and 1960s climbing was done as a way to train for mountaineering. It had a purely adventurous aspect in that virtually nothing had yet been climbed. The pioneers of that era carved out their own routes, discovering what was possible and what they could survive. Gradually, climbing became its own sport but retained an adventurous form. As it continued to evolve, it became more and more specialized, giving rise to sport climbing on popular local crags.

Chris loved the wide open spaces and big rocks that he encountered in traditional rock climbing, where nature in all its glory can be enjoyed in solitude. He found his calling in the pristine climbing marvels of the West, having come of age in the South Platte River Basin—the place he called home. Greg's and Chris's bible was an old South Platte guidebook, and their goal was to climb every notable route in it.

"Chris was a svelte, fluid climber with strength in endurance and mental composure," Greg said. "He could climb all day; the routes that spoke to Chris were long, steep, aesthetic, and the challenge of bold, scary pitches enhanced the sense of adventure." There were spans of rock face without cracks, for example, that had to be crossed without protection—where a fall could be serious—or places where the holds were so slight, a climber could barely grasp the rock. But, as Greg observed, "That is not to say that Chris wanted to get hurt or wanted to die; just that is where his strength lay."

Greg remembered a time when Chris's mental poise helped save the day. "We were climbing the Castle, one of the big rock formations way back in the South Platte. Chris led the really hard pitches to get us up. When we got to the top the wind started whipping like crazy. The clouds moved in, and it started snowing hard, and the next thing we knew it was hailing. The descent was down a steep gully where the anchors to the rappels were farther than the rappel took you, so each time you dropped you had to scramble down the gully to get to the next anchor. It was terrifying! All of the ledges were covered with hail and snow. Moving any distance at all was death defying, because if you so much as slipped, you were going to the bottom. It was in situations like that, that I was always thankful to have Chris with me because he was so encouraging, so supportive, and so not predisposed to complaining or finding the negative. It was all about, *How are we going to do this? Let's make it happen!* He had this resolve that often I did not have at those moments."

It was never just about the thrill of the climb, Greg said, but the entire experience; the choosing of gear, the carrying of a heavy pack—Chris would carry extra weight and rope and really go—often epic approaches requiring hours of arduous hiking and bushwhacking. "Chris didn't have the ego of wanting to be tough. Part of it was training. But really, it was a celebration of the duality of being in a body yet having an unattachment to it. He loved to hike and hurt, feel physical strength and pain, to suffer and endure."

There were also times of simply being. Greg recalled hiking up to the Dome in the South Platte and coming upon a little granite rock garden. "We said, 'Ah, let's take a break.'

We sat down and started throwing rocks, making a game of it, seeing who could hit what first. There we sat for an hour and a half, forgetting the climb, sitting on a hillside enjoying the vista, throwing rocks. Chris could be entertained for hours tossing pebbles."

When I asked Greg what he thought climbing gave to Chris, he said that the journey was always more important than reaching the summit. The destination was rewarding too, but more from the perspective of having savored every last pitch.

"Climbing for Chris was the ultimate expression of being alive in the physical realm. Talk about an activity of concerted movement! Chris often said that what he loved about climbing was the feel of it—the aesthetics of moving across stone. It's like a ballet. On tricky slab climbing, where the rock is less than vertical, you are on precise smears that are barely holding your weight. The thought of falling on slab terrifies me, as you are getting beat up by granite all the way down. I'd rather take a big fall on a steep overhang because it's clean air. Chris excelled at slab climbing; it was his forte. It demands above all calmness, courage, and balance on nearly nonexistent smears and edges. Every muscle is engaged.

"Also, nothing makes you feel so alive as that which points out the frailty of life. There is a quote that lives in me for Chris from a climbing poster that he kept on his wall: *We take these risks not to escape life, but to prevent life from escaping us.* I think the whole notion of mortality and the gift of life intrigued Chris, and the type of climbing he favored reflects that. It required him to step up to his full potential."

Chris, on left, and Greg at the base of Mr. Toad's Wild Ride, after a climb.
Sedona, Arizona, spring 2003.
Photograph © Greg Van Dam, 2009.

The last time Chris and Greg saw each other was in Moab, Utah, just before Chris went on to Yosemite. Chris had asked Greg to join him there. Little did Greg know they were going to climb Moses. Chris had discovered Moses the year before when he was riding the White Rim Trail—a 101-mile mountain bike ride through the Canyonlands of Utah.

"Even before I went out to meet him in Moab, Chris knew what we were going to do. We were going to climb Moses. I'd never heard of it. It's a classic, scary, desert tower, not well known, not well traveled. We took off in Chris's Subaru, a long drive down a crazy road way to the backcountry of Canyonlands.

"It was on that drive that we had the eagle experience. We drove up to this eagle right in the middle of the road— the big golden eagle that Chris chased up the hillside trying without success to take its picture. It would hide behind rocks, move in and out, stop and turn around, then start hopping again, almost encouraging Chris to follow it. Finally Chris gave up and came back to the car. We didn't drive a hundred yards when that eagle, full wingspan, swooshed right over the road and off into the distance. Then we went in and climbed Moses, a magnificent tower, really clean, just a hidden gem. Chris's climbing really shone on that route. It was a hard, hard route. He led the challenging pitches, and we made it to the top."

I thought that Chris, if given the chance, would not go back and do anything differently. From the earliest age, he was always breaking out into new territory, new heights, new vistas—new realms of freedom. You could cherish Chris, but you couldn't contain him. I envisioned him dancing up the sheer silent slopes, the gods of Earth, his gaze anchored in an abiding source.

A few months after that fateful day, I spoke with Michael Lowe, Chris's only climbing teacher. His words remain a comfort to me.

"I remember the giant fourteen-year-old kid and his dad coming into Thrill Seekers, the climbing gym where I worked. They paid, and I gave Chris his first lesson.

"It was very apparent from the beginning that Chris had the psychological foundation to be a great climber. I now know that Chris reached inside himself and made climbing more than just a hobby. He understood it on the level that few of us understand it—that it isn't a hobby. It's a craft. It is an essential part of how we define ourselves.

"I taught Chris to climb, and he died. To this day I don't know how I feel about that. But I take solace in the fact that Chris, by virtue of his personality, did more living than most people. I went to his memorial, and there were all these disparate people of different races and cultures, old, young, men and women. They all had one thing in common. They recognized they had been touched by someone very important. And yes, some were climbers and some were bicyclists, but it was clear that this young man had something we all appreciate. Chris was something that most of us strive to be. He was extraordinarily comfortable inside his own skin. When you meet someone with a strong inner conviction, who seems untroubled by the deeper questions of life simply because they have that kind of faith—you wish you could be that way. The world has people who impact other people, and the experience of meeting one of those people is rare enough that you always remember that experience. Chris was one of those people. In that way, he lives on in a very real sense.

"Ultimately Chris could not be swayed from the direction that he knew was right for him. He wasn't just stubborn; he was confident. He had the confidence that it takes to carve out a successful course and that he could maintain even in the face of criticism and questions from those around him. I think that is what drew people to him. They knew that if no one else knew what was going on, Chris knew. That is another way he will live on. People will look to him in that capacity and try to emulate it. And thankfully that strength of character exhibited itself in someone of Chris's disposition. It was expressed with love and kindness and interest in others."

I also take comfort in these words from Chris's friend Seth Campbell.

"Chris carried with him an air of certainty, as though he completely accepted that he was here. Not that he knew why any more than the rest of us, but that he accepted. He didn't seem to be fighting the eternal struggle of *Why am I here and what should I do?* He was doing it. He died doing it. It would seem that he had found his link to the Earth and the energy that connects all things.

"Mountain biking, skiing, and hiking were the activities that allowed Chris and me to develop a kinship. I would watch him race down a ski slope ahead of me or disappear into the forest on his bike. Because let's be honest: If Chris didn't want you to keep up, you weren't going to. So now that he's gone, why am I still trying? I'm trying because trying is what it's all about. Chris didn't teach me this; he silently encouraged it.

"Is there any more vital characteristic of an exceptional person than humility? I would have never known of some of Chris's adventures had I not asked. He exuded humility, and while he was physically inspiring, it was his humility I admired most. But Chris was not only humble; he had the courage and strength to pursue the dreams and challenges that fulfilled him. I try to incorporate into my own life the lessons learned through knowing him. What good are my feet if I don't walk, my hands if I don't grasp?

"Chris offered a glorious and undeniable example in the way he lived and loved life. I don't remember him as great so much as I remember him as true. Many of us have hopes of 'awakening,' but it is only possible when you release yourself to the possibility. The possibility is life, and life is the possibility of losing everything. I think of Chris often when I'm outdoors. That is his home now. One day it will be mine too."

I recall that night, more than two years ago, when I went up to Breckenridge and met Chris's girlfriend, Tamara, and how thrilled I was, seeing him in love. Not long afterwards Tamara broke up with him. Chris was brokenhearted for a little while; then he let it go. Instead he settled for becoming her best friend.

When I spoke with Tamara after Chris died, I asked her why she broke up with Chris. She said they were in different places.

She was thinking about her future, with marriage and a career, while Chris was thinking about how to make the most of each day. One day she talked to him about her goals. She said she wanted to return to school to pursue her PhD in teaching; then she asked Chris what he wanted to do. With a huge smile Chris had said, "I want to chase the sun."

Tamara told me that after they broke up, Chris would help her. "I was worried about the future, wanting to find someone. He would say, 'Why are you worried? Just live your life. You don't have to look for it. It will come and find you. If it's meant to be, it will happen.' Now I'm engaged, and I wish I could call Chris. I want Chris to know that he was right. You don't have to go looking for it. It will come to you."

The past is remembrance of who we were and the future a promise of who we may be. But truth is in the moment—that which is and will always be. Therein lies the spark of God.

Time is upon us, and everything is timely. This moment is a jewel—my breath, my means, and the ground upon which I stand. That is why Chris was always smiling. For Chris, life was a simple response to a simple offer: *You shall have life, and it shall be yours to live.*

"We can spend our entire lives trying to do good for the world yet the balance of good and bad will remain the same," Chris said.

The good fight emanates from within. Behold the treasure you are. Nothing can keep you from the life that is yours. Stay true to yourself, and your steps will be golden rungs.

The last time I saw Chris he was smiling. He swirled close to the ground in a great big wonderful smile, the smile I've always known. *Look, Mom, at who I have become.* He had climbed his mountain and touched the Sun.

The creative Spirit sends us to life and gathers us home, when all is said and done.

Epilog:
STONE STEEPLE

On a recent spring night, Greg came over for dinner. I asked him to bring Chris's Yosemite climbing guide-book. We opened the guidebook to the page detailing the route where Chris fell, Overhang Bypass on Lower Cathedral Rock. On the map, Greg was able to estimate the location of the fall. Chris fell in an area called "the hog trough," just beneath the ledge he was headed for—where the terrain slackens to an easy grade. The guidebook gives this description of the route:

> Overhang Bypass is taxed by a fairly involved ap-
> proach and descent. The rock is compact and clean-
> ly fractured, the "hog trough" being particularly
> clean and exposed. However, some loose rock is
> also found on the route.

Little by little we reclaim the life that was so disrupted when fate knocked in the night. Little by little I step back into the world. There are things I haven't done for a long time. I have not listened to music in my home or to NPR. I have seen friends, gone to movies, played my grand piano only sparingly. Yet there has been tranquility and comfort. I have relished the quiet and repose.

The time draws near to the third anniversary, and I want to live again. Are there words of wisdom that I might share? Is there some final peace I can make with Chris's passing?

For the first time, I put on a Mozart concerto and turn up the volume.

> *Cry if you must, dear Mom, but don't forget the wind rushing through the hills, the poppies in the field, your shining days. Do not waste them, for the time is short, though our love is long.*
>
> *I fell, Mom, because falling is the only way to live. Haven't you noticed the irony of human fragility coupled with endurance of soul? If we aren't willing to fall, dear Mom, we will never learn. If we aren't willing to let go, we will never know.*
>
> *But Mom, this is what I want you to understand. Come close so I can speak to you in earnest. Beneath appearances, in a truer sense, I didn't fall that day. You don't fall when you are on this flake of time, with focus and balance, listening and responding. There is no room for error. It is a narrow passage, steep and unforgiving. Yet there is great comfort here, great charm. In reality there is no place to fall on this precipice that stretches on and on. You don't fall when you poise on that eternal rim where life unfolds. That's when and where you grow wings. That is how you learn to fly.*

Today is a new beginning. It's time to move on. The May light peeks through my window, the early bird is singing, and the flowers are abloom. All of life comes around yet all is changed, and I must move with the times. I have no choice. Chris will not be with me in the same way, nor I with him. We each have our own path, yet our souls are cut from the same diamond, the same breath, the same God. Always we are one.

What is the pain of a fall compared with the freedom that follows? What is loss compared to the treasure trove of growth that comes in its wake? Who are we but fallen angels by God's grace so that we may pull ourselves up to reclaim our light?

Surely, our visions contain a seed of possibility. Our lives hang in the balance, waiting to get word, waiting for the voice that comes with every breath. It's the moment I've longed for. The one worth living for, the only one I have.

The word I hear today rises on the horizon with Godspeed. *Let go his hand.* This is the peace that I make, my step for now. I feel him soaring. I feel his bliss. *I will never leave you,* he said. And I let go his hand.

Glossary:
CLIMBING TERMS*

Aid climbing: Using climbing gear to help in the ascent, as opposed to using gear only for safety. This type of technical climbing is required when there are no natural rock features to support upward movement, such as footholds and finger cracks.

Anchor: A system usually consisting of two to four pieces of gear that are tied together or equalized, then used to support the climber, who clips his/her harness into the anchor as he/she belays the other climber.

Arête: An outside corner of rock. Usually an arête forms a 90-degree angle.

Belay: A procedure of securing a rope, so if the other climber falls, he/she won't hit the ground. A stationary person feeds out or takes in rope through a device that is attached to his/her harness. In effect, the belayer can pass rope freely through the device to allow the climber to make upward

---

* Most of these definitions are from Greg Van Dam. A few are from other friends, notably Teague Holmes.

progress, or by changing the position of the rope, make the device create so much friction that the rope cannot slide through, and the climber is stopped in a fall.

Carabiner: Forged aluminum ring with a spring-loaded gate through which a climbing rope is threaded. Used to connect to gear placed in the rock or to provide connections to an anchor.

Crack climbing: Climbing in which upward progress depends on using cracks in the rock. A climber twists his/her hands, fingers, feet, elbows, or any other body part to jam in the crack and uses that placement to move up.

Crux pitch: The most difficult pitch on a route.

Free climbing: Using hands and feet on rock features to climb up, unassisted by gear or rope. The rope is attached to the climber, and the climber places gear *only* for protection in case of a fall. In order to move, you need to "receive" the path of the rock, i.e., accept what the rock has to offer and adapt your body and mind to it in order to ascend.

Free soloing: Climbing without a partner, a rope, or any form of aid.

Gear: Equipment the climber anchors to the rock to aid in an ascent (aid climbing) or to arrest a fall only (free climbing).

Hold (foothold and handhold): Natural rock features on which the climber steps and balances or grips by various techniques in order to ascend.

Jam: Wedging hands, fingers, fists, or feet in a crack in order to ascend the rock. Also used as a noun, as in "toe jam."

Lieback flake: A piece of rock partly detached from the wall.

Mantle: Pulling up onto a rock feature such as a ledge or shelf and standing up. The climber pulls on a ledge with both hands in order to lift his/her body, steps a foot very high to reach the ledge, then stands up on it.

Piece: A "piece" of gear (or protection) is placed by a lead climber in a crack; the rope is then connected to the piece via a carabiner. Types include spring-loaded camming devices (cams) and stoppers.

Pitch: A section of climbing. Long routes are broken into pitches. A 300-foot climb will be typically two or three pitches.

Portaledge: Climber's tent that attaches to the side of a cliff.

Protection: See "Gear."

Prusik: A sling attached to the rope by means of a prusik knot, which slides one way and locks the other, used especially in emergency situations.

Rappel: To descend by sliding down a rope which is fastened to an anchor such as a bolt and passed through a device attached to the climber, providing friction. If the wall is vertical or less than vertical (slab), the climber walks or hops backwards, with the feet on the wall for balance.

Runner: A loop of webbing attached between a piece of gear and the carabiner to provide extension.

Runout: A long stretch of climb without gear in the rock.

Slab climbing: The rock face is less than vertical. Climbing slab depends on friction between the climber's feet and the rock, requiring precise footwork and balance over tiny holds.

Smear: Adhering the ball of the foot to a slightly rounded rock feature for friction. Also used as a noun, as in "smears and edges."

Sport climbing: Climbing in which preplaced bolts in the rock are used for protection. The climber clips each bolt with a carabiner and then attaches the rope. Sport climbing is more accessible and generally safer than traditional climbing.

Stopper: Wedged-shaped nut placed in a crack to provide protection in ascending the rock.

Top-roping: A type of climbing in which the rope passes from the climber through an anchor at the top of the route and then to the belayer, who may be stationed below or above the climber. This is generally the safest system of protection, as a fall can be arrested immediately.

Traditional climbing: Climbing in which a lead climber places gear as he/she climbs the rock, which the following climber removes. Generally the routes are longer and more adventurous than in sport climbing.

Acknowledgments

I am indebted to my mom, Julie Hamilton, who is an inspiration, and to my siblings, Bill Richards, Diana Richards, and Kathleen Helmericks, all of whom arrived on the day Chris died and have been with me in love and support ever since.

I thank Greg Van Dam for his invaluable contribution to my understanding of Chris as a climber. My appreciation extends to Teague Holmes for being a guide and companion for part of my journey and for allowing us to see Chris up close on the climb.

To Lincoln Else, I give thanks for the care he took in relating the facts of the accident. I am grateful to Sibylle Hechtel for her skill and courage on the day Chris fell.

My sincere thanks goes to the others whose lives were touched by Chris and who contributed to my knowledge of him—Steve Sharp, Lupe Fabian, Jay Poucher, Chris Pappas, Scott Washowiak, Seth Campbell, Tamara Loveday, Kirk

Addcock, Frank Guerin, Todd Ghorai, Rory Best, Ed Geiss, Paul Young, Chad Pumgerchar, John LeDrew, Mark Long, Eddie Mendez, Michael Lowe, Mike Storm, Buffy Van Dam, Jonny Copp, Kevin Cochran, and Matt Miller.

I am grateful to Chris's dad, Alan, who quite simply was the best dad for Chris. I thank Pauline Goody for the teachings and wisdom that she and the late Shihan Frank J. Goody, Chris's martial arts master, imparted to Chris.

I am indebted to my teacher, Dawn, who opened my eyes to a deeper reality and helped set the stage for receiving Chris's death.

I wish to thank Sara Jenkins, my editor, for the guidance and the gift of discernment she brought to this work.

Photography credits:
Jonny Copp / Coppworks.com, p. 93.
Julie Hamilton, p. 43.
Alan Hampson, p. 29.
Chris Hampson, pp. 6, 74, 78, 117.
Doug Thomson, p. 111.
Greg Van Dam, pp. 25, 52, 141.
Cover photograph of Chris Hampson by Greg Van Dam with Photoshop manipulation by Denise Gibson.

Design by Denise Gibson, Design Den, Spokane, WA.

Carol Hampson was born and raised in Louisiana. She moved to Colorado as a young woman to pursue a career in special education, later moving to the mountains southwest of Denver to raise a family. While her children were still young, she found her professional calling in life as a storyteller, performing original stories as well as myths and legends from world cultures. After attending the Cook Street School of Fine Cooking in Denver, she started her own company, staging dinner/performances for local audiences. In 2003, the sudden loss of her son, Christopher, became the inspiration for writing a memoir. This is Carol's first book.

Access reviews/testimonials or connect with the author at www.morningsongbooks.com.